The Rise of
The Magnificent Mile

Eric Bronsky
Neal Samors

Introduction by Gary Johnson
Foreword by Bill Zwecker

Chicago's Books Press

The identities of the world's greatest cities are often linked to a very special avenue or boulevard. Chicago's is unequivocally North Michigan Avenue. Entering The Magnificent Mile at its Chicago River portal, with the illuminated buildings serving as a backdrop, generates the same sense of wonder and anticipation as crossing the drawbridge leading to a fabled castle. The vista remains as timeless as this 1963 photo (courtesy of the Chicago Transit Authority).

Published in the United States of America in 2008 by
Chicago's Neighborhoods, Inc.

First Edition

Edited by Eric Bronsky, Neal Samors, and Jennifer Samors
Produced by Eric Bronsky and Neal Samors
Designed by Sam Silvio, Silvio Design, Inc.
Printed in Canada by Friesens Corporation

ISBN 13: 9780979789250

Front Cover
Michigan Avenue, looking north from the Chicago River in August,
2008 (courtesy of Golub & Company, photograph by John Caruso).

Back Cover
In 1924, the Allerton Hotel, then one of few tall structures on
Michigan Avenue, served as a perch for this view looking north.
The Water Tower and Pumping Station (foreground) had been built
55 years earlier, but the Fourth Presbyterian Church and Drake Hotel
were relatively new (courtesy of the Chicago Transit Authority).

For more information on this book as well as the authors'
other works, visit www.chicagosbooks.com or email the authors at
EBronsky@aol.com or NSamors@comcast.net.

TABLE OF CONTENTS

To my mother Eleanor, a lifelong Chicagoan
who introduced me to the wonders of Michigan
Avenue at an early age —*Eric*

To my parents, Joseph and Bernette, who always
loved the city, especially the magnificence, beauty
and excitement of North Michigan Avenue and its
surrounding neighborhoods —*Neal*

To generations of Chicagoans, going downtown meant going to the Loop. North Michigan Avenue was not a destination so much as a corridor leading into the central business district. But today our civic leaders can boast that the Greater North Michigan Avenue district and the Loop district, conjoined by a majestic river crossing, *are* Chicago's downtown!

North Michigan Avenue's rise from obscurity to prosperity is a microcosm of Chicago's transformation from hog butcher for the world to world-class city. From its inconspicuous origin as a residential side street, today's bustling avenue is testament to a metamorphosis spanning nearly a century. Our earliest urban planners envisioned the quiet street as a strategic link between North Side lakefront communities and the central part of the city. Many years hence, innovative developers saw its potential as a hub for large mixed-use buildings that combined upscale retail venues with office and residential space. And the work of reshaping this thoroughfare as the axis of one of the world's most prestigious commercial districts continues.

The Magnificent Mile moniker, aptly coined in 1947 by ambitious local developer Arthur Rubloff, became a self-fulfilling prophecy. Today's avenue unquestionably ranks among the greatest thoroughfares of the world's major cities. In fact, its success has not only overflowed to the adjoining Streeterville and Rush Street neighborhoods but has also spawned trendy new neighborhoods—River North, River East, and North Bridge. These thriving localities are becoming ever more vital adjuncts to the greatly expanded downtown.

Looking past the superlatives, economic realities have also shaped the rise of The Magnificent Mile. Skyscrapers replaced many of the quaint low-rise buildings that once characterized the avenue, and high-density developments in turn brought congestion. As costs soared, the mix of retail businesses evolved from local entrepreneurs to ubiquitous national and international chains, bringing a modicum of sameness to North Michigan Avenue. Fortunately a strong sense of local identity prevailed, keeping this a very unique and special place. The avenue's urban geography, architecture, style, and spirit are pure Chicago.

From the restored 19th century Water Tower landmark to the mixed-use Water Tower Place complex, today's Michigan Avenue is a fascinating and stimulating blend of antiquity and cutting-edge modernity whose broad range of compelling attractions draws tourists and residents of all ages. But we also cherish our nostalgic recollections of an earlier time when the avenue was on a more intimate scale. In these pages, we shall rediscover long-gone favorite places like Chez Paree, Charmet's, the Kungsholm Puppet Opera, and the Cinema Theatre. We will also explore some adjacent streets that presented an amazingly colorful contrast to Boul Mich. But mostly we will celebrate the progression of events before and during the 90-year time span from Michigan Avenue Bridge to North Bridge.

Eric Bronsky and Neal Samors

ACKNOWLEDGMENTS

The authors want to express their gratitude and appreciation to Gary Johnson, President, Chicago History Museum, for writing an outstanding introduction to *The Rise of The Magnificent Mile*. It provides the reader with a detailed analysis of how North Michigan Avenue rose from the ashes of the Great Chicago Fire and developed into one of the greatest avenues in the world. Also, we want to thank Bill Zwecker of the *Chicago Sun-Times* and *CBS-2, Chicago* for his brilliant and poignant preface to the book that could only have been written by a lifelong Chicagoan.

We give special acknowledgement to the Greater North Michigan Avenue Association for helping us to shape the book and providing the authors with several outstanding photographs. First and foremost, John Maxson, President and CEO of GNMAA, worked with the authors to identify interviewees, provide support, and assist us in all aspects of this book project. Also, special thanks to Ellen Farrar, GNMAA Vice President of Marketing and Communications, for working with us to identify photographs in the association's collection.

In addition, we want to express our deepest appreciation to those who gave time and support to uncover key photographs for the book. They include Rob Medina of Chicago History Museum, Bruce Moffat and Joyce Shaw of Chicago Transit Authority, Art Peterson of Peterson-Krambles Archive, Lawrence Okrent of Okrent Associates Inc., Justin Snyder of *Opera in Focus*, Bradley Cook of Indiana University Archives/Charles W. Cushman Photograph Collection, Aaron Baker of Playboy Enterprises, and Julia Ayala and Laurie Meyer of Walgreens Co. We also thank Graham Garfield and Walter R. Keevil for their assistance with photographs.

The authors want to express their appreciation to the following individuals who participated in the creation of this book as interviewees, providing us with a wide range of their fascinating, thought provoking, poignant, and personal memories of the Greater North Michigan Avenue District and how it has changed over the years. They include: **Holly Agra**, President, Chicago's First Lady and Chairman, Illinois Tourism Alliance; **Donald Allerton**, Development/Planned Giving/Communications, Fourth Presbyterian Church; **Joel M. Carlins**, Co-Chief Executive Officer, Magellan Development Group LLC; **Grant DePorter**, President, Harry Caray's Restaurant Group; **Tom Dreesen**, Comedian; **Eugene Golub**, Chairman, Golub & Company LLC; **Shecky Greene**, Comedian; **Peter Hanig**, President, Hanig's Footwear; **Christine Hefner**, Chairman and Chief Executive Officer, Playboy Enterprises, Inc.; **Camille P. Julmy**, Vice Chairman, U.S. Equities Realty; **James Klutznick**, Principal, Klutznick-Fisher Development Co.; **Lucien Lagrange**, Principal, Lucien Lagrange Architects; **Larry Levy**, Founder and Chairman, Levy Restaurants and Chairman and CEO, The Levy Organization; **The Honorable Burton Natarus**, former Alderman, 42nd Ward; **Lawrence Pucci**, Custom Tailor and Owner, Pucci, Inc.; **Rick Roman**, Chairman and CEO, The Signature Room at the 95th; **Marc Schulman**, President, The Eli's Cheesecake Company; **Gordon Segal**, CEO and Co-Founder, Crate and Barrel; **Justin Snyder**, Principal Puppeteer and Artistic Director, *Opera in Focus*; **Gail Spreen**, President SOAR (Streeterville Organization of Active Residents) and Real Estate Broker, Streeterville Properties; **Phil Stefani**, Owner, Phil Stefani Signature Restaurants; **Ralph Weber**, Vice President, Northwestern Memorial Hospital; **Abra Prentice Wilkin**, Abra Prentice Wilkin Charitable Trust; and, **Bill Zwecker**, Journalist, *Chicago Sun-Times* and *CBS-2, Chicago*.

FOREWORD

By Bill Zwecker
Columnist, *Chicago Sun-Times*

When Arthur Rubloff coined "The Magnificent Mile" to promote North Michigan Avenue as an upscale destination for shopping and dining in Chicago, he certainly captured the essence of the Windy City's "Champs Elysées" of the late 1940s and early '50s, but that real estate legend accomplished something else—a savvy hint of amazing "magnificence" yet to come.

Thanks to the friendship my mother, *Chicago Daily News* fashion editor Peg Zwecker, had with Arthur Rubloff and his first wife, Jo, I was privileged at an early age to get to know that real estate visionary. Over the years, I became fascinated by Rubloff's canny sense of anticipating public tastes and interests, something he obviously used to his own personal financial advantage. But beyond that, Rubloff was intrigued by everything that had anything to do with the further enhancement of his "Magnificent Mile."

Before I became a journalist full time, I spent about a decade in retail merchandising. Shortly before I was about to launch a small animal-themed gift shop named Animal Accents at 56 E. Walton in 1977 (a half-block west of Michigan Avenue), I happened to be lunching with Arthur Rubloff in his office's dining room. Even though he didn't own the building where I was renting space for the shop—a relatively small 1,800 square feet—Rubloff insisted on reading my store's lease, going over my proposed business plan and first year's sales projections, and even questioned me in detail on the merchandise mix I was planning on showcasing.

The point: Rubloff was deeply interested in anything and everything that was happening on or near the avenue, the stretch of commerce he strongly felt needed to be "the Cadillac" of retailing for the Midwest.

Of course, times have changed greatly, but I can't help but wonder what Rubloff would think, if he were alive today, about the old I. Magnin space being partially replaced by Victoria's Secret and Filene's Basement stores. As a voracious reader, though, he would likely be pleased by the presence of a Borders anchoring a good-sized chunk of the former Magnin's.

While many of my favorite haunts—once popular establishments—are long gone, I still can't walk down Rubloff's Magnificent Mile without remembering places like the Drake Hotel Drug Store's "Americana Room" (ah ... I still remember that wonderful chicken salad!!!), the Diana Court building, Jacque's Restaurant, the Cinema and nearby Esquire and Carnegie theatres, Kon-Tiki Ports, Don the Beachcomber, O'Connell's (with those great long-term waitresses who always called you, "Honey"), or the Kungsholm (and its miniature replica of the Stockholm Opera House, where I celebrated my confirmation as the puppet theatre presented Mozart's "The Magic Flute"). The loss of Stuart Brent's and Carol Stoll's bookshops still saddens me greatly. I also miss Eli's the Place for Steak and being able to drop into Carol and Irwin Ware's fur boutique, just to hear one of Irwin's always amusing tales.

Fortunately, a few places are still alive and well including our favorite media haunt, the Billy Goat. While Riccardo's is gone, its replacement, the wonderful Phil Stefani's 437 Rush, still exudes the same feeling and hence still snares some of our best newspeople— like the *Tribune's* brilliant Rick Kogan—as patrons.

And Ike Sewell has left us, but his Pizzeria Uno (and Due) still tantalizes us with his signature Chicago-style deep dish pizza. Plus, his Su Casa Mexican eatery reminds us of the time when (unlike today) you had a hard time finding good Mexican fare on Chicago's North Side.

Michigan Avenue remains vibrant and alive and truly has become a shopping and dining mecca, not only for Chicago, but for the entire region. It is indeed a very special place.

Michigan Avenue has always been a magical place after dark. The Wrigley Building was illuminated at night beginning in 1921, and the Lindbergh Beacon atop the Palmolive Building was installed in 1930 (photographer unknown, courtesy of the Chicago History Museum, ICHi-52305).

INTRODUCTION

By Gary T. Johnson
President, Chicago History Museum

This book is full of memories, but how was it that Chicago came to have one of the world's grand boulevards, The Magnificent Mile?

As a thoroughfare, The Magnificent Mile is that portion of North Michigan Avenue which stretches three quarters of a mile from the Chicago River on the south to Oak Street on the north. As an area, it also extends a few blocks east to Lake Shore Drive and a few blocks west to State Street. As The Greater North Michigan Avenue Association's wider promotional concept, it extends farther south and west.

What does it mean for a city to have a grand avenue? For one thing, it invites comparisons with other global cities, such as Paris. Columnist Irv Kupcinet often spoke of the Mag Mile as "Boul Mich." The Parisian "Boul Mich," of course, is the Boulevard Saint-Michel—the most famous street in the Left Bank of Paris, but not the most famous street in Paris. That honor belongs to the Champs-Elysées, undoubtedly its grand boulevard and the mandatory setting for parades and ceremonies. This broad, tree-lined boulevard begins and ends with large public monuments in the Place de la Concorde and the Arc de Triomphe. The sightline continues though the Tuileries Garden and to the Louvre, that royal palace that is one of the world's great museums.

In the case of The Magnificent Mile, some of the usual ingredients are missing. It is not a dramatically wide street; compared with Chicago's great boulevard network, such as Logan Boulevard, it only can claim the "boulevard" name metaphorically. With rare exception—most notably, The Magnificent Mile Lights Festival—Chicago's public parades use other streets. Trees are smaller in scale than those lining Martin Luther King Drive and many other Chicago streets. The floral plantings are beautiful, but new. The Mag Mile does not have public monuments; Grant Park has a string of public statuary. None of Chicago's great Museums in the Park have an address on the Magnificent Mile; the closest is the Museum of Contemporary Art, which is a block away. In fact, the only "park" is the little area with trees and benches surrounding the old water works; in any other part of the city, this would be called a playlot. Grand boulevards in world capitals have massive government buildings, but The Magnificent Mile does not even have Chicago's City Hall.

Nobody misses any of these conventional features of other grand boulevards because The Magnificent Mile has its own notable qualities. Coming from the south, the Michigan Avenue Bridge forms a ceremonial entryway, and the way forward is flanked by the Wrigley Building and Tribune Tower, two fanciful and much-loved buildings. Chicago's Water Tower was built for practical reasons, but in the form of a neo-Gothic fantasy. It won its status as a monument the hard way, by surviving the Great Chicago Fire—a battlefield promotion, if there ever was one. Up the block and visible for many miles is the John Hancock Center with all its muscularity, easily many Chicagoans' favorite skyscraper. Just past the Drake Hotel, the Mag Mile falls off into the lake on the north, with drop-dead gorgeous views from Oak Street Beach and North Lake Shore Drive.

Every grand avenue has its own particular menu of uses. In my opinion, the key ingredients of the Mag Mile's menu are these: mixed retail and residential on Michigan Avenue itself, with nightlife nearby and flanked by education, religion, and medicine.

Let's begin with religion and education, the two most surprising elements. If Presbyterians had cathedrals, then Fourth Presbyterian would be it. It has all of the characteristics of a "tall steeple" church—strong endowment, strong membership, and a pulling power for attendance that reaches into the suburbs. Despite its historically strong social appeal with some of Chicago's first families, it prides itself for its work with the poor, including tutoring programs. It sometimes surprises people that the Roman Catholic cathedral, Holy Name, is not downtown in the Loop, but always has been on the Near North Side, just a few blocks west of Michigan Avenue. Saint James Episcopal Cathedral is there, too. Loyola University has a near north campus, which now includes the Loyola University Art Museum—"LUMA." To the east, in Streeterville, is Northwestern University's Chicago Campus, with its medical school and law school. These religious and educational institutions, along with the Newberry Library and the Moody Bible Institute a little farther west, have been neighborhood anchors for decades.

Don't underestimate Rush Street as one of Michigan Avenue's main ingredients. Restaurants and bars bring life to the area and attract visitors from all over the Chicago area. One sign that the Mag Mile truly is a grand avenue is that people come there for a stroll after enjoying dinner in another neighborhood.

The Mag Mile's mix, of course, changes over time. For example, the center of gravity within the educational presence is shifting toward health care as Northwestern Memorial Hospital continues to expand. Locally-owned retail has retreated to less expensive parts of the city; these have been replaced by national and international stores. In some mixed-use venues, such as the John Hancock Center, condos are squeezing out offices. (My dentist still has his office in Water Tower Place, where, surprisingly, there is one floor of professionals amidst the retail, hotel, and condominium complex.)

A grand boulevard, of course, is a construct; it doesn't just happen. It needs to be identified as a destination. But when the concept is established, it exerts a powerful influence over the mind.

Try this experiment: Ask a Chicagoan where he or she remembers seeing the *Cows on Parade*, that wonderful, whimsical outdoor art display back in 1999. The answer invariably will be, "On The Magnificent Mile." True, there were 100 cow statues on the Mag Mile or nearby, but there were 162 at other locations, including the Loop, the airports and, appropriately enough, even the site of the old stockyards. Why do we remember them best on the Mag Mile? Probably because that is where many of us saw them, but that's not all. Our memory places the cows there because of the image that we have of the Mag Mile as our grand avenue. Our memory tells us that if cows were on parade in Chicago, then that's where they must have been.

Surely there is not a more iconic symbol of Chicago's rise from the ashes of the 1871 Great Fire than the historic Water Tower and Pumping Station. Designed by William W. Boyington and completed in 1869, the timeless landmark witnessed the city's rebirth and nearly one and a half centuries of growth and change. At the time of this 1916 photo looking north from Chicago Avenue, this portion of what would eventually become North Michigan Avenue was called Lincoln Parkway (Eric Bronsky Collection).

How can we continue to make our own Magnificent Mile memories? This is my suggestion—a destination that combines the old and the new. Go to 40 East Erie Street, just west of Michigan Avenue. The mansion at that address is the Richard H. Driehaus Museum. Call first because visiting hours are limited.

This museum, which opened in 2008, is a triumphant reminder that once there were Gilded Age palaces on the Near North Side of Chicago, much as there were on New York's Fifth Avenue. Samuel Mayo Nickerson was a distiller and a founder of the First National Bank of Chicago. His "Marble Palace" was built between 1879 and 1883 in what the museum calls "an exuberant mix of Renaissance Revival, Schinkelesque Neo-Classicism, and Aesthetic Movement design."[1] The loving restoration by fund manager Richard H. Driehaus took even longer, from 2003-2008. A new laser technique meticulously scrubbed the blackened exterior to restore its original vibrancy. The interior marble, woodwork, tile, and glass are breathtaking, but make no mistake—this is no mere monument to the details of Nickerson's life and possessions. This is a living museum, with a living patron, one with his own exuberant

generosity and taste. The Nickerson mansion now is the home to holdings from the Driehaus decorative arts collection. As they say in the world of real estate, "Watch this space!" My guess is that every visit will be rewarded with a new treasure on display or another splendid room opened to the public.

Above all, the world's grand boulevards are places for walking. That's where the memories are made. Start anywhere at all on The Magnificent Mile and stroll the length of the street, up and down, and then back again. This mile and a half will not take long, even if you wander off the street, east or west, a block or two. You will rub shoulders with those who live in this great neighborhood, or come from other parts of the city or the region. You can be sure that just about every international visitor to Chicago will do the same. (Check international websites and blogs, and you'll see what I mean!)

This book is full of those memories, of those who helped to shape The Magnificent Mile and those who simply enjoyed it, but the best memories will be the ones that you make yourself.

1 Driehaus, Richard H. and M. Kirby Talley. The Richard H. Driehaus Museum. Chicago, 2008. (Afterword by M. Kirby Talley).

following page
The topography traversed by Michigan Avenue is shown in this aerial photo taken in March 2007. Chicago's central area appears as four quadrants, with the Chicago River Main Branch as the east-west axis and Michigan Avenue as the north-south axis. Clockwise from left-center are Grant Park and Lakeshore East, Chicago's downtown Loop district, the River North neighborhood, and Streeterville/River East (photo by Lawrence Okrent).

North Michigan Avenue looking north from Grand in August, 1957.
Nearly all of the buildings in this view date to the 1920s.
A Pixley & Ehlers restaurant stood at the corner of Michigan and
Ohio. (J. Sherwin Murphy photo, courtesy of the Chicago History
Museum, ICHi-52301)

Fifty years later, how things have changed! The Woman's Athletic Club of Chicago building (identified by its mansard roof), the Water Tower, and, of course, the Allerton Hotel (partially hidden behind the 625 N. Michigan building) are among the few remaining 1920s-era buildings, now dwarfed by modern skyscrapers (Eric Bronsky photo).

The Michigan Avenue Building, located at the northeast corner of
Michigan and Ontario, was still bordered by old mansions and
walkup apartment buildings as of June 1935. The taller building in
the background was the Eastgate Hotel (Hedrich-Blessing photo,
courtesy of the Chicago History Museum, HB-2788-B).

Now home to British retailer Burberry Ltd., this same corner
building along with the former Eastgate Hotel are now dwarfed by
soaring office and hotel towers (Eric Bronsky photo).

The Michigan-Chestnut building, seen under construction in 1928, combined retail space on two lower floors with office space above. Retail tenants through the years included Colby's furniture store and the first Michigan Avenue location of Crate & Barrel (Aerial Photo Service Inc., courtesy of the Chicago History Museum, ICHi 23417).

The Michigan-Chestnut building was demolished in 1992, and its replacement is the retro Plaza Escada, designed by architect Lucien Lagrange to emulate the Parisian style and scale espoused by Daniel Burnham. Park Tower (left) and the 111 E. Chestnut Condominiums dominate the background (Eric Bronsky photo).

The block-long street between Chicago and Pearson, immediately west of the Water Tower, was known variously as Tower Place and Tower Court. In this 1905 view looking north from Chicago Avenue, the mansions facing Water Tower Park were then among the most prestigious addresses in Chicago. In later years, the corner building at far left housed the Normandy Restaurant (*Chicago Daily News* photo, courtesy of the Chicago History Museum, DN-002477).

Circa 1955, the short street was officially renamed North Michigan Avenue. Today, Park Tower and Loyola University's Lewis Towers offer unparalleled views of the historic Water Tower Park. Facing the park on Pearson are the Bistro 110 restaurant and the Ghirardelli Chocolate Shop, both located in the former Bonwit Teller building (Eric Bronsky photo).

below

The south side of Chicago Avenue between Michigan and Rush, shown in 1976, supported a hodge-podge of small but quaint buildings with local businesses. The whimsical Ballantine's was originally Rickett's Restaurant (Sigmund J. Osty photo, courtesy of the Chicago History Museum, ICHi 29721).

right

The multi-faceted 730 N. Michigan Avenue development revitalized an entire square block, a prime location whose prior use had been marginal at best. Today, the luxurious Peninsula Hotel occupies the Rush Street side of the block between Chicago and Superior. Facing Chicago Avenue are trendy boutiques and a café. In the fall of 2008, American Girl Place relocated from here to Water Tower Place (Eric Bronsky photo).

The diminutive but elegant 543 N. Michigan Avenue building with its Parisian and Art Deco design elements epitomizes the architectural style of buildings on the avenue in the 1920s (Trowbridge photo, courtesy of the Chicago History Museum, ICHi-31314).

Perhaps on account of its small footprint, the 543 building was not a prime candidate for redevelopment. Its restored facade now houses Nokia's Chicago flagship store (Eric Bronsky photo).

Part 1
Bridging a Divided City
1837–1920

The "old-world" ambience of Pine Street, before its makeover into North Michigan Avenue, is deftly captured in this image looking north from Illinois Street (Eric Bronsky Collection).

Harold F. McCormick, son of Cyrus Hall McCormick, acquired this aquatint engraving, titled "Rush Street Bridge Chicago in the Year 1861," back in 1930. It was displayed in the McCormick mansion at 675 N. Rush Street until the house was emptied after World War II (Eric Bronsky Collection).

Chicago's earliest visionaries set their shovels and axes to fertile soil along a pristine lakefront and with the ability to expand in three directions on flat land with no natural boundaries other than the river. With Fort Dearborn strategically situated along the south bank of the river near its confluence with Lake Michigan, the fledgling town logically began to develop on the same side of the river as the fort, spreading south and west. The city of Chicago was incorporated in 1837, and subsequently, a tract of land known as the Fort Dearborn Addition was platted. The name given to the easternmost roadway shown on that early diagram was Michigan Avenue—Michigan is derived from a Native American word meaning "great water."

Located just yards from the shoreline, the earliest predecessor to today's world-class avenue was at first nothing more than a nondescript dirt road with a few wooden houses. But Chicago grew exponentially during the first half of the 19th century, and the burgeoning population rapidly built upon this vacant land, then expanded across the main, north, and south branches of the Chicago River. The area south of the river evolved as a commercial district, and the tract north of the river, originally known as Kinzie's Addition, became primarily residential.

As the new city expanded, so did the need to get people and goods back and forth across the river. The ferries dating to the original pioneer settlement were soon outmoded, but the shippers who depended on navigable waterways vehemently protested anything that might obstruct the river, particularly bridges. Following dissent, progress prevailed and the first movable bridges, built during the 1830s, were primitive affairs constructed of lumber. In 1849, a disastrous flood swept away all of the early bridges and center-pier swing bridges were gradually built to replace them.

In June 1856, the city hired civil engineers Harper & Tweedale to design and build a swing bridge, the first iron bridge in the west, across the river at Rush Street. Just six years later it was destroyed by a cattle stampede. Ironically, the wooden truss bridge that replaced it perished in the Chicago Fire just a short time later. The rebuilding that was hurriedly completed in 1872 also proved woefully inadequate and was replaced by a fourth Rush Street bridge in 1884.

Completion of the initial river crossing at Rush made Kinzie's Addition more attractive to potential residents. What would eventually become the northward extension of Michigan Avenue was originally known as Pine Street

between the river and Ontario Street, and north of Ontario it was called Lincoln Park Boulevard, later Lincoln Parkway. In those years, it was a relatively quiet and narrow residential side street. Many of the new homes built here were large mansions with elaborately landscaped grounds. The growing prosperity of the new neighborhood in turn attracted businesses catering to the elite. The developing waterways and railroads enabled local merchants to bring in an array of items that was remarkably sophisticated for what up until then had been a frontier town.

The Water Tower and Pumping Station, destined to become Michigan Avenue's most compelling historical icons, were designed by William Boyington and built between 1867 and 1869. Practically the only buildings to survive the Great Fire of 1871, they came to symbolize Chicago's strength, resilience, and spirit. Following the fire, reconstruction began in the central area almost immediately, but it took nearly a year for the building boom to work its way north of the river. Large residences, mansions, and elegant family hotels then sprang up rather quickly. Several members of the McCormick family colonized the area around the intersection of Rush and Erie Streets and built spectacular residences; citizens wryly dubbed the neighborhood west of Pine Street "McCormickville."

The focus of early commercial development in Chicago was unquestionably south of the river, where tracks of the nation's sprawling railroad network converged at several large terminals ringing Chicago's central business district. Additionally, the street railways and, starting in the 1890s, elevated trains that delivered people to the Loop, were an important factor in State Street's stellar rise as Chicago's main retail corridor.

In contrast, the only form of transportation north of the river and east of State Street before the automobile age was horse-drawn vehicles. So, what would eventually become the Michigan Avenue corridor was effectively isolated from the central business district. Significant retail migration would not occur until many years later. Nonetheless, the focus of social life in the city gradually shifted north, with McCormickville and the Gold Coast becoming more fashionable for residential development than Prairie Avenue on the Near South Side.

Lake Michigan used to lap near the foot of what is now the north approach to today's Columbus Drive Bridge. From there, the shoreline tapered northwesterly to just east of the Water Tower and Pumping Station, and then continued to its present alignment north of Oak Street. But investors and real estate speculators managed to convince the city to construct breakwaters and add 120 acres of landfill to expand the area east of Pine Street for development. This area became known as Streeterville, named for the capricious boat captain who tried to claim the sandbar acreage as his own after his schooner ran aground in 1886.

Not every change was progressive, for urban planning as we know it today was still in a primordial stage. West of the prosperous lakefront neighborhood, the Clark Street corridor was evolving into a seedy stretch of men's hotels, saloons, and cheap amusements. As factories and warehouses rose along the north bank of the river, the axis of residential development shifted north of the Water Tower towards the Gold Coast, away from the riverfront commotion and congestion. Development of the unsightly three-block stretch of Michigan Avenue between the river and Randolph Street stagnated on account of the adjacent South Water Street Market, railroad yards, and warehouses.

The first proposals for major improvements to Michigan Avenue and Pine Street emerged during the 1880s. The World's Columbian Exposition of 1893 was being planned, and the city sought to showcase its central area and Gold Coast to the many anticipated visitors. It was generally agreed that Pine Street should be widened between Chicago Avenue and the river, and more importantly, that this thoroughfare should connect to the central business district by either a bridge or underground tunnel. But this topic grew into a hotbed of ongoing planning and debate. Further delayed by the question of financial support and then the required passage of ordinances, construction would not actually commence until some 25 years later.

The World's Fair was a celebratory and pivotal event for Chicago. It launched the idealistic City Beautiful movement championed by architect Daniel Burnham, who sought to emulate the classical flair of the great European cities by introducing the monumental and ornate Beaux Arts architectural style to Chicago. "The White City," as the Fair's landscape of grand exposition halls was dubbed, inspired not only a new architectural movement, but more significantly, cohesive urban planning and renewal.

As Chicago segued into the twentieth century, its prosperous downtown bulged at the seams and the need to create a new link between the Gold Coast and the Loop grew critical. The limited capacity of Rush Street Bridge created serious bottlenecks, made worse by the frequency of its openings for river traffic. Moreover, the center piers of swing bridges greatly restricted the allowable width of vessels entering the Chicago River, posing a serious navigational hazard. Replacement of all such outmoded structures with double-leaf Scherzer and then bascule type bridges, which afforded a much wider channel, began in earnest in 1894.

Various civic groups proposed designs for a new Michigan Avenue bridge, but the project picked up considerable momentum once The Commercial Club of Chicago, founded in 1877, endorsed and supported Burhnam's utopian City Beautiful vision. It was the club that underwrote the innovative 1909 Plan of Chicago. Authored by Daniel Burnham and Edward Bennett, the Plan was an ambitious long-term program to revamp and beautify Chicago's infrastructure, thereby improving the city's image to the outside world and the quality of life for its residents. An artist's rendering accompanying the Plan depicted Michigan Avenue as a wide boulevard emulating Paris' pedestrian-friendly Avenue des Champs-Elysées with its landscaped plazas and walkways, enhanced by dignified architecture whose size did not overwhelm the scale of the thoroughfare.

Considering that Michigan Avenue would be a key component of the Plan, the authors wrote:

"In considering the Heart of Chicago as a single composition it is desirable to begin with the base line. Obviously this is found in Michigan Avenue... So desirable has this thoroughfare become that extensions of it to the north or the south must enhance the value of the abutting real estate.

Michigan Avenue is probably destined to carry the heaviest movement of any street in the world. Any boulevard connection in Michigan Avenue which fails to recognize the basic importance of the avenue will be a waste of money and energy. Any impairment of the capacity of this street at any point along its entire front, any weakening of this foundation, is an error of the first magnitude.

This great improvement will come because it is a part of a plan which provides a basis of street circulation, and which will weld and unify the three detached sides of Chicago; because it will improve facilities for commercial traffic, and at the same time preserve for the people the uninterrupted use of their greatest and most attractive highway."

In 1912, the North Central Business District Association (known today as the Greater North Michigan Avenue Association) was established to represent local interests and work with civic leaders in transforming Burnham's vision to reality. Charles Wacker, an enthusiastic proponent of the Plan, was campaigning to replace the squalid South Water Street market along the south riverbank with a two-level roadway. He advocated building Michigan Avenue Bridge and approaches on two levels to intersect the proposed east-west roadway. This would make it possible to segregate delivery and service vehicles on a separate level from automobile and pedestrian traffic, thus reducing congestion and improving safety. The upper level roadway approaches would span over east-west streets and freight railroad trackage, and would have the added benefit of necessitating the modification or replacement of the decaying loft buildings flanking the roadway.

Even though the City Council passed an ordinance to permit the new project and a bond issue was approved to fund it in 1913, the process of acquiring and condemning property to permit the widening of Michigan and Pine delayed the actual start of construction until 1918. Once begun, though, work was completed within two years and Pine Street/Lincoln Parkway officially became North Michigan Avenue.

As envisioned, the May 1920 opening of the new bridge and the widened avenue represented much more than a symbolic joining of the two halves of the city. This majestic new thoroughfare was a gateway that would attract investment and development, ushering in a new era for the growth and prosperity of Michigan Avenue.

The Robert A. Kinzie residence, photographed in the 1860s, stood on the northwest corner of Austin (now Hubbard) and Rush. The attached greenhouse and ornamental woodwork hint at prosperity (photographer unknown, courtesy of the Chicago History Museum, ICHi-14155).

The post-fire years saw a rapid rebirth of the area surrounding the Water Tower as a neighborhood of fine homes of comparatively fire-resistant construction. This delightful "castle" at the northwest corner of Lincoln Parkway and Erie was built circa 1875 for Theodore Sheldon (photographer unknown, courtesy of the Chicago History Museum, ICHi-52290).

Following the Great Fire of 1871, all that remained of the second Rush Street Bridge were its stone piers. A replacement was hastily erected using the existing piers (Eric Bronsky Collection).

The opulent John V. Farwell residence, designed by Burnham & Root and completed in 1882, stood at the northwest corner of Lincoln Parkway (Michigan) and Pearson. Farwell owned one of the largest wholesale firms in the country. Borders Bookstore occupies this site today (photographer unknown, courtesy of the Chicago History Museum, ICHi-52299).

"Many of the people who built up Chicago after the Great Fire came from outside of Chicago. Potter Palmer, Marshall Field, Samuel Insull, and others came with that 'I Will' spirit and built up a new city within a very short time. And we're only now waking up to the fact that today's Chicago does not belong to just one ethnic group or one race." *Lawrence Pucci*

Samuel Nickerson, founder of the First National Bank of Chicago, commissioned this grand mansion at 40 East Erie Street in 1883. Magnificently restored to its Gilded Age splendor, this building is now the Richard H. Driehaus Museum (photographer unknown, courtesy of the Chicago History Museum, ICHi-01251).

An early non-residential structure was the castle-like armory building for the 1st Cavalry Illinois National Guard. Built in 1907, it stood on Chicago Avenue east of the Pumping Station. Later enlarged, it was demolished in 1993; the Museum of Contemporary Art stands on this site today (*Chicago Daily News* photo, courtesy of the Chicago History Museum, DN-0071256).

Not all residential buildings were of the same high caliber. This building, located at 418 N. Pine Street circa 1903, was alleged to be a gaming house (*Chicago Daily News* photo, courtesy of the Chicago History Museum, DN-0001412).

Bicycling has always been a favorite Chicago pastime. On a hazy day in 1901, a crowd of cyclists and spectators gathered for a race in front of the Water Tower. (*Chicago Daily News* photo, courtesy of the Chicago History Museum, SDN-000523).

The quiet nature of the residential neighborhood prior to the North Michigan Avenue era is captured in this view of Lincoln Parkway looking north from Erie on May 14, 1911. The Water Tower is visible in the distance (Watriss photo, courtesy of the Chicago History Museum, ICHi-52292).

top left

Horse-drawn wagons of Belden Manufacturing Co. and W. C. Reebie & Bro. wait patiently to cross the swing bridge at Rush Street circa 1911. Note that no physical barrier existed to prevent vehicles or pedestrians from plunging into the river other than a wig-wag signal with the warning, "Bridge Danger" (Eric Bronsky Collection).

bottom left

The richly adorned Medinah Temple, completed in 1912, housed a 4,200-seat auditorium. Many concerts and events, notably the annual Shrine Circus, were held here through the years (Hedrich-Blessing photo, courtesy of the Chicago History Museum, HB-04858-A).

top right

Looking west on Ohio from Cass (now Wabash), to the right, is the Judge Lambert Tree residence. When this photo was taken in 1911, the home was about to be demolished to make way for construction of the new Medinah Temple (*Chicago Daily News* photo, courtesy of the Chicago History Museum, DN-0056745).

bottom right

The Medinah Temple building today exemplifies adaptive reuse. Its landmarked exterior has been faithfully restored; however, the interior was gutted and rebuilt. Since 2003 it has housed the Bloomingdale's Home Store (Eric Bronsky photo).

Across the river, the three-block stretch of North Michigan Avenue between the river and Randolph was sandwiched between the South Water Street Market and the Illinois Central Railroad, and lined with factories and warehouses. This 1911 view looking north from Randolph shows a cigar store on the corner (J & B Moos photo, *Chicago Daily News*, courtesy of the Chicago History Museum, DN-0057273).

Donald Allerton

The Fourth Presbyterian Church was formed on February 12, 1871 from the merger of two congregations on the north side of the Chicago River, North Presbyterian Church and Westminster Presbyterian Church. Although there were by then churches in Chicago named Fifth, Sixth, Seventh, Eighth, and Ninth, the name Fourth was not in use. Perhaps it had been given to a church that did not succeed in organizing. As it turns out, the North Church, organized in 1848, had been the fourth Presbyterian church to be organized in the city.

Over the summer of 1871 they renovated the larger of the two buildings, which was located at Grand and Wabash where Nordstrom is today. They worshipped in their new church home on Sunday, October 8, 1871. That night, at about 9:00 P.M., the Great Chicago Fire destroyed 18,000 buildings, including the new Fourth Church. All but five families lost their homes, and the pastor found refuge in a pumpkin patch on the north side of Fullerton.

In 1872, the trustees of the church purchased a lot at the northwest corner of Rush and Superior as a site to build a new church. The completed building was dedicated in February 1874 and served the congregation for 40 years. In 1911, the Michigan Avenue (then unpaved Pine Street) site was purchased and the Gothic style building was dedicated on May 10, 1914—the first important structure built on what was to become The Magnificent Mile.

Except for the Old Water Tower, Fourth Church is the oldest building on Michigan Avenue north of the Chicago River. The architect was Ralph Adams Cram of the firm Cram, Goodhue and Ferguson from Boston. Cram's reputation was established by winning a worldwide competition to design the chapel and master plan for West Point in 1903. He was considered America's leading Gothic Revival architect, best known for his work on the world's largest Gothic cathedral, the Cathedral of St. John the Divine in New York City. Charles Connick, also of Boston, is responsible for all the stained glass. He was known for his ability to replicate the cobalt blue stained glass for which the Gothic Cathedral of Chartres, France is known.

As plans for the new Gothic building were unfolding, church member Cyrus Hall

McCormick announced that the McCormick family would contribute $1 for every $2 raised by others. The McCormicks lived in the neighborhood, and their son Harold Fowler McCormick and his wife, Edith, John D. Rockefeller's daughter, lived in a 41-room mansion at 1000 North Lake Shore Drive.

As for my background, I relocated to Chicago when I was recruited here by a major pharmaceutical company. Then, for 26 years, I served as the founding partner in an executive search consulting firm. I've been a member of Fourth since 1976, and in 2001 I gave myself permission to retire early. Since "retiring," I have served as a full-time volunteer filling various interim roles with the church. I also volunteer as a career coach at the Career Transitions Center of Chicago and serve on the board of the Presbyterian Historical Society, which oversees the archives for the denomination.

The Fourth Presbyterian Church calls itself "A Light in the City" with outreach programs that touch every constituency in the city and a spirit of hospitality and inclusivity. For example, during World War II, a controversial decision was made to provide space for a Japanese-American congregation to worship despite restrictions imposed on them during the war years. That tradition of being a welcoming and serving community continues to this day.

By the end of the twentieth century, the Fourth Presbyterian Church had become a landmark institution on North Michigan Avenue, known today as The Magnificent Mile. Thousands of visitors pass through the church's doors to find an oasis of calm, take in the beauty of the building, hear a summer concert, or to just find sanctuary there.

North Michigan Avenue literally grew up around Fourth Presbyterian Church. Completed in 1914, only the Water Tower and Pumping Station have existed longer than this cluster of Gothic Revival buildings, whose serene courtyard offers pedestrians a welcome respite from the noise and crowds of the avenue (courtesy of the Chicago Transit Authority).

On Friday, April 7, 1916, at about noon, Lincoln Parkway was practically deserted except for a column of well-dressed people, all strolling south past the Water Tower. Perhaps they were parishioners heading home after a funeral or other special service at Fourth Presbyterian (John R. Taylor photo, Eric Bronsky Collection).

The Avenue in 1916

In preparation for street widening and constructing long ramped approaches to the new Michigan Avenue Bridge, the surveyors photographed all of the properties about to be modified or condemned. Hundreds of highly detailed images, taken with a large-format view camera between February and June of 1916 and mounted on linen, were eventually placed in storage and then forgotten. Only some 65 years later, when City workers emptied the contents of a dusty storage room into a Dumpster, did this remarkable photographic record finally emerge from obscurity.

In addition to views looking north and south along the thoroughfare, the surveyors also photographed building facades from the opposite side of the street in such a way that entire blocks of buildings could be visualized by arranging the photos in sequence. Digital technology now makes it possible to merge these photos together almost seamlessly into panoramas that accurately depict how entire city blocks appeared in 1916. With the exception of the Water Tower and Pumping Station, none of these buildings exist today.

Prior to completion of Michigan Avenue bridge in 1920, the stretch between the river and Ontario Street was called *Pine Street*. The stretch from Ontario to Oak Street was known over time as *Lincoln Park Boulevard* and *Lincoln Parkway*. *Austin Avenue* is now Hubbard Street and *Cass Street* was re-named Wabash Avenue.

All photos are from the Eric Bronsky Collection.

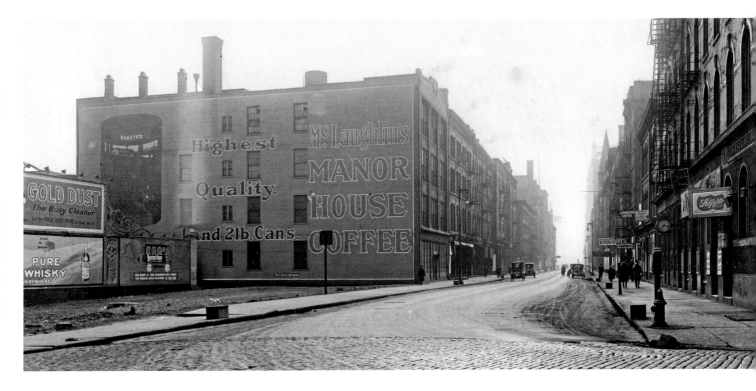

East side of Michigan Avenue, south of the Chicago River

A view of Pine Street, looking north from
Austin Avenue (now Hubbard Street).

River Street, looking northwesterly towards Michigan Avenue. The extension of East Wacker Drive was eventually built on this site.

River Street

E South Water Street

E South Water Street

Lake Street

Lake Street

Randolph Street

West side of Pine Street and Lincoln Parkway,
north of the Chicago River

Austin Avenue   Illinois Street

Illinois Street   Grand Avenue

Grand Avenue   Ohio Street

Ohio Street to Ontario Street

Ontario Street

Erie Street

Erie Street to Huron Street

Huron Street to Superior Street

Superior Street to Chicago Avenue

Lincoln Parkway, view south from Chicago Avenue

Pine Street appeared bleak and deserted on a frigid winter day before the start of the widening project. The buildings on the left side of this view looking north from Ohio were condemned and about to be vacated (Charles Barker photo, courtesy of the Chicago History Museum, ICHi-04489).

Widening of the avenue finally commenced during 1918 with demolition of the buildings on the west side of Pine between the river and Chicago Avenue. This view looks north from Ontario (*Chicago Daily News* photo, courtesy of the Chicago History Museum, DN-0070180).

An agile photographer presumably climbed to the top of the Water Tower for this view looking north towards Oak Street just before the start of construction of the Drake Hotel. The John Hancock Center, Westin Hotel, and Palmolive Building would eventually fill in the vacant land along the east side of the avenue (photographer unknown, courtesy of the Chicago History Museum, ICHi-52289).

Two views of the bridge over the Chicago River at Rush Street, built in 1884, during its final years. Looking northwest from the intersection of Michigan and River (now East Wacker Drive), it's obvious that Rush Street was not aligned with Michigan Avenue—traffic had to negotiate a sharp jog and then jockey for position onto the narrow bridge (John R. Taylor photo, Eric Bronsky Collection).

Pedestrians were allowed to remain standing on the swing bridge when it opened for river traffic, something that is not possible on today's bascule bridges! (Frank W. Hallenbeck photo, Eric Bronsky Collection).

In preparation for a link-up with the new Michigan Avenue Bridge, the widening and ramping of the three-block stretch of Michigan Avenue from Randolph Street to the river was mostly completed by the time of this September 1919 photo (J.J. Johnson photo, Eric Bronsky Collection).

Part 2
Upper Boul Mich
1920–1947

A 1922 publicity photo of the recently completed Michigan Avenue
Bridge highlights the brand new Wrigley Building South Tower in the
background. This, the first split-leaf double-deck trunnion bascule
bridge ever built, was an engineering triumph and the realization of a
long-term goal to separate delivery and service vehicles from
automobile traffic. With the addition of sculptures to the four bridge
towers during 1928, the bridge became a monumental gateway
between North Michigan Avenue and the Loop district
(Eric Bronsky Collection).

The buildings that "anchor" the four corners of Michigan Avenue
Bridge were designed to enhance the perception of the bridge as a
gateway. In November 1924, both the Wrigley Building North Tower
and Tribune Tower were under construction (Chicago Architectural
Photographing Company, Eric Bronsky Collection).

The dream of linking the Loop district to the Near North Side, and the many years of haggling and planning before the first spade of earth was finally turned, created high expectations. Contemplating rapidly escalating property values in tandem with the expansion, investors and developers launched an unprecedented building boom. In fact, the construction of several major new buildings was underway well before the avenue project was completed.

The disorganized nature of the post-fire era rebuilding had taught civic leaders the lesson of careful planning. The tasks of creating and implementing standards fell to the North Central Business District Association, whose members concurred that this thoroughfare would be more viable as an upper-echelon business district. Over the next decade, most existing residences and neighborhood businesses were replaced by grander edifices housing banks, office buildings, first-class hotels, and exclusive shops. The automobile showrooms, warehouses, factories, and saloons that prevailed south of the river would not be welcomed here.

The stretch of Michigan Boulevard south of the river had been referred to as Boul Mich, so it seemed appropriate to dub the newly extended avenue north of the river Upper Boul Mich. This moniker was surely consistent with the Parisian-style thoroughfare depicted in Plan of Chicago renderings. But although designers and planners promoted an esthetically pleasing melding of architectural styles and sought to limit the maximum heights of buildings, developers anxious to maximize the return on their investments ultimately won the cooperation of the City Council. The city's first comprehensive zoning ordinance, adopted in 1923, paved the way for the rise of skyscrapers along the new avenue with no cap on total height.

By the mid-1920s, Michigan Avenue was well on its way to becoming a thoroughfare of unique and special stature. The mix of low-rise and high-rise structures with varied architectural styles surely diverged from the uniformity that the early designers called for. However, many of these buildings were outstanding works of architecture in their own right. The new bridge, with a quartet of office towers anchoring its corners, and the majestic new Drake Hotel at the opposite end of the avenue, effectively established gateway or "portal" entrances to the newly created avenue. Then as now, these structures are at once bold and brawny, yet stately and elegant. They create a visual excitement and a sense of anticipation that enhances the stature of the blocks in between.

As the axis of central business district growth and development shifted northward, well-established South Michigan Boulevard boutiques like Peck & Peck began to open new stores north of the river. The success of the new shopping district lured New York's famed Saks Fifth Avenue to Chicago in 1929. Luxury stores, restaurants, and hotels catering to Chicago's elite gradually displaced neighborhood residents and businesses who could no longer afford the escalating rents. A colony of artists, their enclave of studios, antique shops, and coffee houses called Towertown on account of close proximity to the Water Tower, gradually dispersed to less expensive neighborhoods. But the early presence of this bohemian culture had a palpable influence on Michigan Avenue's reputation as a gathering place for cognoscenti and as a milieu for the fine arts.

The building boom continued through 1929, at which time the stock market crash and the ensuing Great Depression, followed by World War II, halted further expansion. Indeed, several businesses along the avenue filed for bankruptcy, and some major buildings went into foreclosure. But the momentum spurred by the redevelopment of Michigan Avenue during the previous decade and the affluent nature of the area compared to other city neighborhoods carried many businesses through the difficult times.

Although no significant new construction occurred during the next two decades, new businesses continued to open up along Michigan Avenue and adjacent streets, where rents were lower. It was in 1935 that Ric Riccardo opened his legendary restaurant on nearby Rush Street. In 1943 he partnered with Ike Sewell, who is widely credited as inventor of the deep dish pizza, to open Pizzeria Uno. The Art Moderne Esquire Theatre on Oak Street welcomed its first patrons in 1938. Meanwhile, women's boutiques like Sydney Korshak and Blum's Vogue migrated here from the South Loop. Clearly Michigan Avenue was poised to resume its ascent as soon as circumstances became more favorable.

top left

Temporary bridge houses were erected so that the upper level of Michigan Avenue Bridge could be opened to traffic on schedule. On May 14, 1920, city officials held a gala ribbon-cutting ceremony replete with band music and fireworks. While this was going on, workmen were feverishly completing the lower level (J. Sherwin Murphy photo, courtesy of the Chicago History Museum, ICHi-29306).

top right

The G&M (Graham & Morton) Great Lakes steamer, *City of Grand Rapids*, delighted onlookers as she sailed beneath the raised Michigan Avenue Bridge. The date was August 30, 1922, and the vessel was carrying a load of passengers bound for Michigan (Eric Bronsky Collection).

bottom right

In this 1921 view of the avenue looking south from the Water Tower, the only building of significant size is the Wrigley Building South Tower barely visible in the distance (photographer unknown, courtesy of the Chicago History Museum, ICHi-04497).

A 1922 publicity photo looking north from Randolph Street shows off a newly widened Michigan Avenue enhanced by boulevard-style streetlights and a mix of new and remodeled buildings. Auto traffic has increased significantly (Eric Bronsky Collection).

top left

The construction boom expanded south across the river with completion of the London Guarantee and Accident Company Building (left) and the Bell (now Old Republic) Building (right). Visible in the distance of this 1925 view are the Michigan Avenue Bridge, Wrigley Building, Allerton Hotel and Tribune Tower (Kaufmann & Fabry photo, courtesy of the Chicago History Museum, ICHi-52287).

top right

This view of the London Guarantee Building illustrates how smoothly its architectural style melds with the design of the bridge (Eric Bronsky Collection).

right page top

The rise of many new buildings and increased density on Chicago's Near North Side within a nine-year time span is evident in comparing these two photos. Besides the Water Tower and Pumping Station, prominent features of this 1924 aerial view include the Fourth Presbyterian Church, Drake Hotel, and numerous smaller residences (courtesy of the Chicago Transit Authority).

right page bottom

The same view in June 1933 is dominated by the Palmolive Building and several high-rise apartment buildings that replaced smaller residences (Ken Hedrich photo, Hedrich-Blessing, courtesy of the Chicago History Museum, HB-01660-A).

top left
Originally built as the Illinois Women's Athletic Club, this 17-story building at 820 N. Michigan Avenue (then Tower Court) was completed in 1927. In 1946, philanthropist Frank J. Lewis donated this building to Loyola University to become their Water Tower campus (photographer unknown, courtesy of the Chicago History Museum, ICHi-52295).

top right
The same view in 1948, little changed, shows a streetcar operating eastbound on Chicago Avenue (Joe L. Diaz photo, Peterson-Krambles Archive).

bottom right
And here is the exact same view in 2008. Perhaps it's appropriate to reintroduce the "Towertown" moniker, as today's impressive new Park Tower towers over Lewis Towers and the old Water Tower (Eric Bronsky photo).

"Upper Boul Mich" had progressed much further by 1927. On the left side of this view looking north from Grand is the Michigan-Ohio building, completed in 1924, and the steel framework for the Woman's Athletic Club of Chicago. On the right are the Allerton Hotel, also completed in 1924; and the Lake Shore Trust and Savings Bank of 1922 (Kaufmann & Fabry photo, courtesy of the Chicago History Museum, ICHi-34495).

The prestigious 900 N. Michigan Avenue building, completed 1927, was noteworthy as the only apartment building built on the avenue during the 1920s (Fred J. Mimkes photo, courtesy of the Chicago History Museum, ICHi-52298).

top right

Holabird & Root's striking Palmolive building, as seen from the Fourth Presbyterian Church, was completed in 1928. Though a considerable distance from the Loop, it nonetheless attracted some important tenants. This view shows the building before the Lindbergh Beacon was installed (courtesy of the Chicago Transit Authority).

bottom left

The Erskine-Danforth building, also known as the Decorative Arts building, was previously a warehouse that architect Philip Maher extensively renovated. Home to the Arts Club of Chicago since 1951, it was demolished in 1995 to clear the way for the mixed-use 600 N. Michigan building (Hedrich-Blessing photo, courtesy of the Chicago History Museum, HB-829-c).

bottom right

The close proximity of a Cities Service gas station to the Water Tower is symbolic of the rise of the automobile as the dominant form of transportation along the avenue. Less prominent buildings were sometimes recognized for popular tenants; such was the case of the building at the southwest corner of Michigan and Chicago. In earlier years it housed The Tailored Woman, a fashionable boutique, but in later years it was best known for Charmet's Restaurant. (*Chicago Daily News* photo, courtesy of the Chicago History Museum, DN-0085047).

The Woman's Athletic Club of Chicago building, located at the
northwest corner of Michigan and Ontario, is shown shortly after
completion in 1928. Some 80 years later, the club remains the
principal tenant in this French-influenced architectural landmark
designed by Philip Maher (Hedrich-Blessing photo courtesy
of the Chicago History Museum, HB-242).

Chicago's skyline changed dramatically during the boom years of the 1920s, with several new skyscrapers rising on North Michigan Avenue and in the Loop district (background). In this view looking southwesterly from the Palmolive building, the Water Tower is in the bottom foreground. Note the much smaller scale of buildings along Rush Street, which parallels Michigan Avenue to the right (*Chicago Daily News* photo, courtesy of the Chicago History Museum, ICHi-18889).

Like a grand finale orchestrated by Chicago's leading architects, the decade of the 1920s closed with the completion of at least seven significant buildings along North Michigan Avenue just in 1929 alone. The Michigan Square Building, also known as the Diana Court Building for its famous Art Deco atrium emulating the style of the great transatlantic liners, fell to the wrecking ball in 1978. The Marriott Downtown Chicago Magnificent Mile Hotel occupies this site today (Hedrich-Blessing Photo, courtesy of the Chicago History Museum, HB-2890).

The Michigan-Superior Building was one of the avenue's earlier examples of a mixed-use structure; it combined retail shops, a recital hall and practice rooms for musicians, artists' studios, and a penthouse apartment complete with a domed observatory! Neiman-Marcus occupies this site today (Hedrich-Blessing photo, courtesy of the Chicago History Museum, HB-05383B).

The elaborate Medinah Athletic Club, shown under construction during 1928, had a varied career. Built as a Shriners private club, it subsequently passed through the ownership of several hoteliers. In 1961, then-owner Sheraton added a modern tower immediately north that featured the Kon-Tiki Ports restaurant, remembered for its elaborate South Seas decor. In 1990, the hotel reopened, beautifully restored as the InterContinental Chicago (photographer unknown, courtesy of the Chicago History Museum, ICHi-19462).

Holabird & Roche's 333 N. Michigan Avenue masterpiece was the last of the four skyscrapers to be constructed adjacent to the bridge. This view looking south shows the close proximity of Michigan Avenue to the Illinois Central Railroad freight yard and warehouses. A pedestrian plaza occupies the site where the east extension of Wacker Drive would eventually be built (Eric Bronsky Collection).

Lawrence Pucci

My father was born in Buenos Aires, Argentina, but he and his family moved back to their home town of Florence, Italy when he was eight. Then in 1911, his family decided to move to America because Italy was drafting young men to fight in the Italo-Turkish War and he was the only son. Life in America was so different back then. It was not yet a 'smokestack' country; 90 percent of the land was still being farmed and the schools taught things like cooking, sculpture, art, poetry, books, and philosophy. My father learned art and design as a youth in Italy. He had a very creative and artistic bent, which he would use to build the family business.

Located on the second floor of the 333 N. Michigan Building with a commanding view of the cityscape, custom tailor Pucci Inc. is the patriarch of North Michigan Avenue local businesses, having operated here continuously since 1929. The prominent gold Pucci emblems in windows facing north and west have been a familiar sight to pedestrians crossing Michigan Avenue Bridge for several generations (Eric Bronsky photo).

He wanted to see all of America, so that's how he eventually made his way to Chicago. While here, he met a beautiful woman named Emma Louise Boissy. They got married, and then my sister Caryl and I came along. My mother was Scottish and English, and her father was French. Her family came here from Montreal, Canada right after the Chicago Fire, so they were firmly entrenched here by the time she met my father.

My father opened his first tailor shop in 1920 at Jackson and Monroe. He started out making clothes for my mother's family, her uncle, and her brothers. The business grew into a fashion design studio employing 30 tailors. He had a wonderful personality, and as time went on he made a lot of friends. You know how people from another country tend to band together with their own kind? Well, although my father was Italian, all of his school friends were Irish and Jewish! So he had an innate ability to blend in with a clientele of different nationalities.

In 1928 he moved his shop to the then brand new 333 North Michigan building. He was the first tenant here, and we've been at this location ever since. It's a great building! On the first floor where Fannie May Candies is now, there used to be an auto dealer that sold Duesenbergs, Cords, and other makes right on the premises. They had an apparatus that removed a window so you could drive the car right out to the street. There were duplex apartments on the top floors. And we were members of the Tavern Club, which closed only recently—we would go up there to watch the parades that came down Michigan Avenue; it was like a reviewing stand. The Civil War veterans even marched in those days.

Just like our country's northern and southern states were completely different, so were North and South Michigan Avenue. Originally the carriage trade and the finer shops and businesses were all located south. Where Columbia College is today used to be the Blum Building, named for Blum's Vogue. Many fine women's clothing shops were located in that building; today they would call it a mall. As time went on, Michigan Avenue developed north of the bridge. Some good stores like Stanley Korshak opened there in the 1930s.

During the war years, a woman planted a victory garden on the site where Water Tower Place would eventually be built. On the same block you could also play tennis, and there was a gasoline station. After the war, a New York ad agency erected big billboards on the site. Blum's Vogue expanded, opening stores on North Michigan Avenue and in Evanston, and other stores soon followed them to the avenue.

Growing up, I lived on Sheridan near the Edgewater Beach Hotel. In the 1920s, we moved closer to downtown to an apartment building on Chestnut. After graduating from Northwestern, I started law school but then I was drafted. On account of my allergies—I had hay fever and asthma—I didn't have to serve. I helped my dad out while waiting for law school to reopen. And that's how I got into my father's custom tailor business; I never returned to law school!

So, we've been serving clients from this same location continuously for 80 years! We built our reputation on craftsmanship by hand, using the finest materials, and we prefer to call ourselves architects of fashion for living legends. My father passed away in 1965, but it's fortunate that my sister and I were able to carry on.

top left

The avenue's prim and stately persona endured through the difficult times. In this 1936 view at Ohio Street looking north, note the architectural similarities between the Woman's Athletic Club of Chicago and the Farwell Building on the next block (Fred G. Korth photo, courtesy of the Chicago History Museum, ICHi-52288).

top right

Early in the Depression era, the avenue became eerily quiet. This scene looks north from Superior (Raymond Trowbridge photo, courtesy of the Chicago History Museum, ICHi-21560).

bottom left

Two construction projects already underway at the time of the 1929 stock market crash were completed during the following year. One was the Union Carbide and Carbon Building (today the Hard Rock Hotel) south of the river, and the other was the Cinema Theatre at 151 E. Chicago Avenue, shown before its marquee was installed. This popular art film house closed in 1981, but the marquee is preserved at the Chicago History Museum (photographer unknown, courtesy of the Chicago History Museum, ICHi-52260).

Traveling to the Avenue

Long before Chicago paved its first road or laid any rails, the waterways were its superhighways. The Chicago River served as an intercity port from the city's early years through the mid-twentieth century. Vessels providing scheduled passenger service between Chicago and various points in northern Illinois, Wisconsin, and Michigan docked along the river's Main Branch; their ticket offices and boarding areas were readily accessible to Rush Street and later North Michigan Avenue.

But the main destination for the majority of boat and railroad passengers was the Loop. Michigan Avenue was a late bloomer, in part because the main transportation arteries radiating outward from the Loop district bypassed this area. The avenue began to emerge as a commercial district only after the business districts of most other Chicago neighborhoods and several adjacent suburbs had already been established.

The city's rapid transit and street railway infrastructure, largely in place before the turn of the century, never provided a truly direct link between the Loop area and what was until 1920 a comparatively quiet neighborhood. By the time the new corridor opened, the private automobile was already becoming popular, and thus autos and buses reigned as the dominant forms of transportation along the avenue.

In the fledgling years of Upper Boul Mich, city residents and visitors typically did not own private motor vehicles. For residents of the Gold Coast or Rush Street areas, this locale was walking distance or else a short taxi ride away, but most people living further out relied on public transportation. Street railway routes for the most part followed the city's familiar grid pattern of north-south and east-west streets, so someone traveling to the avenue from, say, the Loop would ride a streetcar north and then transfer to an eastbound car or else walk the few blocks to Michigan Avenue.

North-south streetcar routes operated along State, Clark, and Wells Streets. Additionally, the main elevated rapid transit trunk route to the North Side ran above Wells and Franklin Streets, several blocks west of the Michigan Avenue corridor. Although none of these routes served Michigan Avenue directly, at Chicago and Grand Avenues riders could transfer to east-west streetcar routes that took them to the avenue.

A bus route linking the Loop with the far North Side, traversing the Michigan Avenue and Lincoln Park corridor en route, was finally made possible by the new Michigan Avenue Bridge. The Chicago Motor Coach Company was the original operator of bus routes along the lakeshore that were subsequently acquired by the Chicago Transit Authority. The opening of the State Street subway in 1943, with stations at Chicago and Grand, further improved access to this area.

Transportation-related projects in more recent years focused on improving vehicular access. An improved connection with Lake Shore Drive at Oak Street and the Ohio-Ontario feeder connection to the Kennedy Expressway were major milestones. As the avenue grew in popularity and traffic congestion increased, new rail transit routes directly serving the area were once again considered but tabled due to lack of funding. During the summer months, Wendella has been providing scheduled water taxi service along the river between Michigan Avenue and Chinatown with intermediate stops, a throwback to an era when river transportation reigned.

below

Street railway service began on Chicago Avenue in 1859 and Grand Avenue in 1875 with horse-drawn streetcars. Both routes were converted to electric streetcar during 1895 and 1896. This 1918 view shows the east end of the Chicago Avenue line at Lake Shore Drive. The brand new Municipal Pier is visible in the distance. The crowd was gathered for an appearance by Billy Sunday, a popular baseball player turned evangelist (*Chicago Daily News* photo, courtesy of the Chicago History Museum, DN-0070057).

bottom

In 1916, several decades before planners would conceive of linking Ohio Street to an expressway, Red Crown Gasoline at 109 E. Ohio was merrily dispensing fuel from a single portable curbside pump at the then exorbitant rate of 20 ½ cents per gallon. The Michigan Square building and, later, Marriott Hotel were built on this block (Eric Bronsky Collection).

above

Streetcars were the dominant form of public transportation on Chicago Avenue for nearly a century. This 1932 view shows an eastbound car rolling across Michigan Avenue (courtesy of the Chicago Transit Authority).

top right

In a scenario familiar to today's CTA commuters, riders jam a Chicago Motor Coach Co. bus on a subfreezing morning in 1926. Open-top buses were pleasurable during the warmer months, but in inclement weather, standees huddled on the rear platform even when there were empty seats on top (courtesy of the Chicago Transit Authority).

bottom right

As Michigan Avenue increased in importance as a retail and business center, Chicago Motor Coach Co. (and later CTA) added and fine-tuned service to meet demand. Soon, a variety of routes that tapped the lake-front and other North Side neighborhoods converged on the avenue. Commuters living along Addison and Diversey enjoyed a one-seat ride to The Magnificent Mile (courtesy of the Chicago Transit Authority).

In 1952, Chicago Avenue east of Michigan was still a "neighborhood" street characterized by modest buildings and family-owned businesses. Walgreens, with its soda fountain, was a popular hangout, and next door was the Cinema Theatre. Madame Galli's, which first opened on Illinois Street in 1893, was the oldest Italian restaurant in Chicago. A sign on the Tower Garage advertised the nearby Younker's Restaurant, famous for its "chicken in the rough" (George Krambles photo, Peterson-Krambles Archive).

The Chicago Surface Lines maintained an enormous fleet of colorful wood and steel streetcars that lasted into the CTA era. A westbound Chicago Avenue car boards passengers at State Street in 1952. It's hard to believe that today's up-and-coming River North neighborhood was once a gritty backwater of dilapidated apartment and loft buildings (H.M. Stange photo, Peterson-Krambles Archive).

In this 1952 view, a car is westbound on Chicago Avenue. The Pearson Hotel in the background would eventually be demolished to clear the way for Water Tower Place (H.M. Stange photo, Peterson-Krambles Archive).

Chicago Avenue cars used to turn south onto Lake Shore Drive and continue to a terminal at Navy Pier, but in 1937, the route was cut back to Chicago Avenue. Here, a car prepares to cross over to the westbound track while an eastbound car waits its turn. The massive armory building is prominent in the background (William E. Robertson photo, Eric Bronsky Collection).

Long before Grand Avenue was converted to one-way, streetcars clanged in both directions under Michigan Avenue. This 1930 view shows a westbound car traversing the eventual site of The Shops at North Bridge (Robert V. Mehlenbeck photo, Peterson-Krambles Archive).

When this photo was taken in 1948, the Pier served as the main Chicago campus of the University of Illinois. In an earlier era, you could actually ride a streetcar out to almost the far end of the Pier (James J. Buckley photo, Peterson-Krambles Archive).

The Broadway route operated via State Street, serving the Rush Street and (indirectly) Michigan Avenue corridor. In the CTA era, streamlined PCC streetcars nicknamed "Green Hornets" ran on this route. This mid-1950s view looks north from the intersection of State, Rush and Cedar (William E. Robertson photo, Eric Bronsky Collection).

Here is the same location in 2008. Streetcar service on the Broadway route was converted to motor buses in early 1957 (Eric Bronsky photo).

The streetcar lines operating on Chicago and Grand were converted
to trolleybuses in the early 1950s. A westbound trolleybus pauses
at the Water Tower during the mid-1960s. The then new Water Tower
Inn is in the background. All of CTA's trolleybuses were replaced
with motor buses by or before 1973 (courtesy of the Chicago
Transit Authority).

Holiday decorations adorn the Water Tower on a bright November
1958 day as a southbound CTA bus pauses at Michigan and Superior.
Bonwit Teller's flagship store is visible behind the Water Tower
(Charles Cushman Collection, Indiana University Archives P10366).

This view looking towards the Wrigley Building and Tribune Tower from the intersection of Wacker and Wabash is remarkable because it was photographed in 1941—color photos from that era are quite rare (Charles Cushman Collection, Indiana University Archives P02386).

The safety island at the same intersection was reconfigured during a recent rebuilding of Wacker Drive. The elaborate cast-iron light standards are long gone. Otherwise the drama of this approach to The Magnificent Mile is intact (Eric Bronsky photo).

A branch of the Chicago & North Western Railway once ran along the north bank of the Chicago River to Navy Pier, serving several industries and warehouses. The Wrigley Building, Tribune Tower, and Medinah Athletic Club are of course recognizable, but virtually all of the other buildings in this 1945 view have been replaced. The Mandel Building, just beyond Michigan Avenue Bridge, was a warehouse that later served as the temporary Chicago Public Library. Wabash Avenue Bridge and the substructure of the new State Street Bridge, whose completion was delayed by the war, appear in the foreground (Charles Cushman Collection, Indiana University Archives P02955).

The Kungsholm Miniature Grand Opera

Today's *Opera in Focus* does not serve smorgasbord but otherwise they maintain the Kungsholm tradition, right down to the sign on top of the proscenium (Eric Bronsky photo).

Michigan Avenue's reputation as a family destination stemmed in part from an elegant Swedish restaurant that thrived for 30 years at the northeast corner of Ontario and Rush. It wasn't the traditional Scandinavian smorgasbord that drew international attention and fame to the Kungsholm so much as a very special and unique form of entertainment. Housed in a ballroom on the fourth floor of the former Leander Hamilton McCormick mansion was a miniature opera house whose performers were mechanical puppets controlled from beneath the stage. These elaborately costumed puppets, predating the technological marvel of animatronics by several decades, were remarkably sophisticated for their time. Manipulated by skilled puppeteers, they could emulate a wide range of human motion and emotion in synch with audio recordings of actual operatic singers.

The Kungsholm Restaurant was just a memory by the time Justin Snyder was born, but he was fortunate to befriend and learn this art form from William B. Fosser, who was closely associated with the Miniature Grand Opera through a two-decade time span. The pioneering Michigan Avenue family attraction lives on today through Fosser's *Opera in Focus* in Rolling Meadows, Illinois, where Justin currently serves as principal puppeteer and artistic director.

A Kungsholm-era puppeteer adjusts the costume on one of the opera's extensive collection of figures. The rods and controls that enabled these puppets to articulate are visible here.

A performance of Giuseppe Verdi's Aida during the early years of the miniature opera boasted elaborate costumes, sets, and lighting that emulated their full-size counterparts. (both photos courtesy of *Opera in Focus*).

Justin Snyder

Although I was born in Salt Lake City, I have spent the bulk of my life in Chicago. I was probably around four or five the first time I visited Michigan Avenue with my mom. All I can really remember is being overwhelmed by the size of the buildings and wanting my mom to buy me toys!

The first I learned of the old Kungsholm Restaurant was in a book on puppetry I'd borrowed from the Mount Greenwood library as a kid. My grandfather, who was a gifted operatic tenor in his youth, had a huge collection of orchestral records that he'd let me listen to after school, so I'd already developed a love for opera by that time. I'd also been fooling around with puppets for years, so I was intrigued to find an art form that combined both of my loves into one craft.

Years later, I was perusing local puppetry websites when I stumbled upon the website for *Opera in Focus*, which is the last remnant of the Kungsholm tradition. At that time, they were actively seeking apprentices to help keep the art form alive, so I contacted Bill Fosser, the producer. That was seven years ago. I have been working there ever since.

Although the Kungsholm closed before I was born, Bill Fosser, who became my best friend and mentor, worked for the restaurant at three different time periods during his career. He started in 1943 when he was only 14, and became artistic director of their Miniature Grand Opera in the early sixties. He left only because the Fred Harvey Group, which bought the restaurant in 1960, didn't want to invest the necessary funds towards maintaining the countless puppets, props, and scenic elements which were all in dire need of major restorative work. Bill went on to a successful career in the motion picture industry, working as a set designer and art director for many films, but in his free time, he continued to perfect the puppet opera as an art form.

Actually it was Ernest Wolff, his mother Esther, and their friend Fred Stouffer who invented the unique rod-puppet opera art form back in 1930. In 1941, a restaurateur named Frederick Chramer purchased the McCormick Mansion and converted it to the Kungsholm Restaurant.

Chramer was a wise man with an imitable talent for spotting something special and elaborating upon it in lavish, opulent ways. When he saw a performance of Wolff's puppet opera that was touring the Midwest, he negotiated an agreement to install their puppet opera in the new restaurant...this was a brilliant move. Sadly, the Wolffs parted company with Chramer in 1947 and a fire destroyed the puppet opera that same year, but Chramer built a new theatre at ground level and encouraged Bill Fosser to return for the puppet opera's grand re-opening in 1950.

Bill single-handedly kept the art form alive after the Kungsholm closed in 1971. Many of our audience members think we're simply using the same puppets they saw as kids at the Kungsholm, but that's not the case. A lot of the original puppets were stolen and others were donated to the Museum of Science & Industry, where they were displayed until recently. In any event, we have a collection of original Kungsholm puppets at our theatre but they are in pretty poor shape due to not being maintained properly towards the end of the Kungsholm's existence. They stand 14 inches tall and are actually quite crude compared to the puppets that we use at *Opera in Focus*. Since they're no longer in a condition that any puppeteer worth his salt would consider "performance worthy," they've all been retired. The *Opera in Focus* puppets are 16 inches tall and are capable of much more lifelike movements than the Kungsholm puppets, even in their heyday.

top left

The L. Hamilton McCormick residence at the northeast corner of Rush and Ontario, as it appeared in 1910, was destined to become the home of the Kungsholm Restaurant and its unique puppet opera (courtesy of the Chicago History Museum, CRC 1330).

top right

In 1941, a ground floor addition was built onto the former residence to provide more space for the restaurant. This view shows Kungsholm as it appeared in 1954 (J. Johnson Jr. photo, courtesy of the Chicago History Museum, ICHi-52263).

bottom right

Kungsholm closed in 1971. After a stint as Shipwreck Kelly's, the building became Lawry's The Prime Rib in 1974. The top two floors of the mansion were damaged during construction of the adjacent building and had to be removed. Otherwise, Lawry's has restored and maintained the building's splendor. Historical memorabilia from Kungsholm is displayed inside the restaurant (Eric Bronsky photo).

Bill began designing the *Opera in Focus* puppets in the thirties, although he didn't actually make the first batch until 1956. Many of the puppets we use today are over 50 years old—we're always building new ones, too—and they move today as effortlessly and gracefully as they did back when Bill first made them. They're the only puppets of their kind in the entire world, and there's no dollar amount that could coax us to sell a single one! Backstage, what looks so seamless and refined from the audience's perspective is actually very complicated and chaotic. Aside from puppeteers manipulating the puppets, our stage area is filled with all sorts of equipment, control consoles, and special effect devices that we utilize in our performances. Nothing is automated...EVERYTHING is done by hand. After every performance, we invite our audiences on a backstage tour to see how everything is done. Bill wanted people—especially kids—to see that our performances are done not by robots, but by highly skilled artists who specialize in every aspect of the craft we practice.

As chaotic as things can get backstage, there are these moments of perfect serenity where everything in the world ceases to exist except for the scene being played out on stage. Bill taught us early on to identify with the role our puppet is portraying, regardless of its age, sex, lifestyle, etc. If the puppet I manipulate is an old gypsy woman, I need to turn off my own thoughts, feelings, and identity and BECOME that old gypsy woman for the performance to be authentic. At times, our puppeteers get so caught up in their roles that it's not unusual for them to weep during highly emotional scenes. It's a beautiful but exhausting thing, both physically and emotionally.

Bill Fosser passed away in early 2006, but he entrusted my brother Shayne, also an apprentice, and me to keep this art form alive. Today, *Opera in Focus* is the only rod-puppet opera in the world, and for us it's a labor of love. Our audiences consist primarily of senior citizens—people who visited and loved the Kungsholm in their youth. When people come backstage with tears in their eyes and thank us for bringing back nostalgic memories of their childhood visits to the Kungsholm, and when young people who have never experienced live theatre or music drama before tell us that after seeing us perform they've developed an interest in studying puppetry and opera; it makes all of the effort we put into keeping this art form alive more than worthwhile.

Everything in this world is constantly changing these days, and I tend to prefer how things used to be "way back when." Many Americans seem to have lost touch with the magic that the performing arts can bring to their lives. Puppetry is still thriving as an art form in other parts of the world, but children here are more interested in things like video games and computers. Let's face it, it's easier to seat a kid in front of a DVD player than it is to put your coats on and go outside in search of magical experiences with them. Even though Kungsholm has been gone for nearly 40 years, it lives on in the minds and hearts of the people who were there and experienced its magic firsthand. The lasting impression that it made on people is apparent to us after every performance! The experience of watching our puppet opera today is the same as when it first began...entertaining, educational, and a unique experience that you won't find anywhere else in the world.

Part 3
The Rise of
The Magnificent Mile
1947–1970

The monumental icons that have come to symbolize Chicago's growth and prosperity are recognized around the world. Undoubtedly this timeless vista, little changed over the course of 80-plus years, inspired Arthur Rubloff's vision for North Michigan Avenue's future. Only the vehicles and fedoras betray the fact that this photo dates to November 1948 (Charles Cushman Collection, Indiana University Archives P04151).

Generations of residents and visitors have flocked to Michigan Avenue to enjoy its annual tradition of festive holiday lighting. This view looks north towards Ontario Street in December 1961 (courtesy of the Chicago Transit Authority).

As the nation's economic development recovered following World War II, Michigan Avenue stirred with the prospect of rebirth. The new appeal of this area to investors and developers was initially spurred by developer Arthur Rubloff, who had the foresight to acquire several blocks of prime real estate at bargain prices and then draw up an ambitious plan to revitalize the avenue. He promoted his plan, a combination of new construction, renovation of existing buildings, and landscaping, as *The Magnificent Mile* project.

In retrospect, it was not the specifics of Rubloff's plan as much as his contagious optimism and brilliant salesmanship that fueled the avenue's revitalization. Rubloff went on to achieve remarkable success with other major real estate projects, notably Carl Sandburg Village. But The Magnificent Mile nickname was indelible, enduring through the avenue's gradual ascent into a premier fashion, commercial, and hospitality center.

During the 1950s, migration to the suburbs and other socioeconomic changes began to negatively impact Chicago's central area. As regional shopping malls sprang up, the vitality of the Loop as a retail and entertainment district began to fade. In contrast, Michigan Avenue north of the river enjoyed a relatively stable concentration of affluent residents in neighboring Streeterville and the Gold Coast, which helped to maintain the aura of a safe haven for both carriage-trade retailers and neighborhood businesses. Property values and rents here remained relatively modest by postwar inflation standards, and astute entrepreneurs saw the avenue as a potentially lucrative site for their businesses. Block after block of street level frontage was enhanced by a pedestrian-friendly blend of stores including Walgreens, Woolworth's, inexpensive snack shops, and airline ticket offices together with trendier restaurants, art galleries, jewelry stores, and boutiques. It should be noted that the majority of retail businesses at that time were locally owned.

The postwar abundance of private automobiles benefitted the avenue by providing convenient access from other city neighborhoods and the suburbs. Lake Shore Drive's connection to Michigan Avenue at Oak Street served as both a convenient and dramatic entry point for motorists.

Construction of the Prudential Building launched Chicago's downtown building boom in the mid-1950s, but on Michigan Avenue north of the river, new high-rises did not begin to spring up until the early 1960s when the Equitable Building rose on the site of an open-air parking lot across from the Wrigley Building. By the end of that decade, nearly all of the remaining undeveloped lots were brimming with new construction. With the notable exception of the Water Tower, Pumping Station, and Fourth Presbyterian Church, the few remaining pre-1920 buildings were replaced.

Probably the most significant turning point was construction of the 100-story John Hancock Building, known today as John Hancock Center. Begun in 1965 and completed in 1970, this skyscraper was initially derided by critics for being out of synch with its surroundings—its unabashedly bold design and overwhelming scale clashed with Burnham's vision, and there was concern that its presence would have a negative impact on the character of Michigan Avenue. Instead, this muscular new tower quickly became an iconic symbol of Chicago that attracted overwhelmingly positive attention. Visible from afar, it drew people to Michigan Avenue, and its observation deck became one of the city's most popular tourist destinations. Combining office, residential, and retail space, it was successful as the first large-scale example of a mixed-use project in Chicago.

Admittedly the character of the avenue had begun to change even before the X-braced tower became a staple of the skyline. Michigan Avenue had reached a figurative crossroads: its future development boiled down to the question of whether economic growth should take precedence over the harmonious balance advocated by the Burnham and Rubloff plans. A compromise was needed.

top left

A sign heralding the demise of the once-stately Poole residence at 645 N. Michigan Avenue symbolized the end of an era. By the early 1950s, the last few mansions remaining from the bygone Pine Street/Lincoln Parkway era were being cleared away (Frank E. Rice photo, courtesy of the Chicago History Museum, ICHi-21327).

bottom left

Retail development along Michigan Avenue resumed with the gala opening of this Moderne style Walgreens store at the corner of Michigan Avenue and Chicago Avenue on September 22, 1947 (courtesy of Walgreen Co.).

top right

Woolworth's built a spacious one-block-deep store at Michigan Avenue and Huron Street with an auxiliary entrance on Rush Street. Today the Omni Hotel occupies this site (photographer unknown, courtesy of the Chicago History Museum, ICHi-52286).

bottom right

Newly-elected Chicago Mayor Richard J. Daley presided over a ceremony upon the completion of a major rehabilitation project for Michigan Avenue Bridge in 1955. The city's role in diligently maintaining infrastructure was crucial towards ensuring the avenue's success (courtesy of GNMAA).

Abra Prentice Wilkin

I was born in 1942 on the South Side of Chicago and after some early years in Lake Geneva, WI, moved back to the Near North Side and have been there ever since. My parents were John Rockefeller Prentice, the grandson of John D. Rockefeller, and Abbie Cantrill Prentice of Freeport, Illinois, who met at the law firm of Sidley & Austin where they both worked.

I attended the Latin School of Chicago for four years until I went away to prep school and college. I retuned to Chicago, attended Northwestern University, and worked for the *Chicago Sun-Times*, and still live in the same apartment on East Lake Shore Drive that my parents bought in 1958. Prentice Women's Hospital is named in honor of their many years of service to Northwestern Memorial Hospital.

Growing up on the Near North Side/Gold Coast was full of adventure, and I have so many memories of my early years there.

As a strictly raised but adored only child, I was not allowed to venture too far from home ("60610 Land," though it was before zip codes), and I instilled similar rules for my own children, who grew up on East Lake Shore Drive (zip code 60611). Outside certain boundaries lurked "stranger danger" and places not fit for young kids. After Old Town made its mark, the boundaries were extended west to include Wells Street.

Oak Street Beach was off limits in the '50s because of polio, which all parents were convinced was contacted where large crowds gathered. Instead, we swam indoors at the nearby Chicago Avenue YWCA on weekdays with the Latin School. Even in later years, that beach was always a little ominous and I rarely ventured there even though it was just across the streets. Maybe it was the underpasses, also a bit spooky!

Like today, North Michigan Avenue was a great place to shop, walk, and feast. There were shoe stores like Andrew Geller (my first pair of patent-leather stilettos) and A.S. Beck's, where we'd get cheap shoes to dye to match our formals or bridesmaid dresses. Then there was Jax, a trendy spot, Shaxted's, and Franklin Bayer for wonderful linens. Our wardrobes came from Blum's Vogue, Stanley Korshak, and Saks when it was on the east side of the street. I remember that I opened up my first savings account for $50 at the Upper Avenue National Bank, and I later banked at the one in the Wrigley Building. Both banks are now gone, as is the Wrigley Building Restaurant where ad men and journalists alike had three-martini lunches.

My first byline at the *Chicago Sun-Times* was covering the topping out of the Equitable Building, and I recall how it seemed to take forever when they were putting in the caissons to begin construction of the John Hancock Building.

Other memorable Michigan Avenue haunts were the Women's Exchange, which had everything; Dorothy Hale for antique wedding presents; Jacques for lunch with its outside courtyard and fortune teller; or Don the Beachcomber and the Imperial House for dinner. And, let's not forget the Allerton Hotel's Tip-Top-Tap where they broadcast the Don McNeill Breakfast Club across the country. I can also recall drinking scorpions at Kon-Tiki Ports, as well as swimming in the pool at the Sheraton Chicago Hotel. My kids and I used to take swimming lessons at the Woman's Athletic Club (WAC), and it is a wonder to me that the club has survived all of these years.

Of course I'll never forget dining at the London House the night of the big blizzard of 1967, and the next day walking to work down a deserted Michigan Avenue in feet of white fluffy snow.

top left

By the 1950s, Michigan Avenue's evolution into a fashion center was beginning to erode State Street's dominance. The 700 N. Michigan building, completed in 1929 and known as the Judah Building, stood at the northwest corner of Michigan Avenue and Huron Street. Chicago Place was later built on this site (photographer unknown, courtesy of the Chicago History Museum, ICHi-30496).

bottom left

Swank shops with eye-catching window displays and awnings beckoned to pedestrians strolling along the attractively landscaped avenue. The Italian Court building is on the right in this 1950 view looking north towards Ontario Street (Dr. Frank Rice photo, courtesy of the Chicago History Museum, ICHi-23102)

top right

Another 1950 photo looking south from Grand Avenue captures the charm of the pedestrian way, the monumentality of the skyscrapers, and the banality of the billboards (photographer unknown, courtesy of the Chicago History Museum, ICHi-52302).

bottom right

Guests staying at the Allerton Hotel had a commanding view of the Water Tower, Palmolive Building, and Oak Street Beach in 1949. They could shop at larger department stores such as Saks Fifth Avenue or Bonwit Teller (at left), and also browse the numerous smaller but interesting shops along the avenue and intersecting streets (W.C. Radebaugh photo, courtesy of the Chicago History Museum, ICHi-52297).

Marc Schulman

My father Eli was born in Chicago in 1910. When he was only 16 years old, he had to drop out of high school when his father, a baker, died suddenly. My dad sold shoes, worked in politics, and then opened his first restaurant in 1940 on the West Side at Ogden and Kedzie. It was within a year of the opening that my dad joined the Army Air Corps, rising to the rank of Staff Sergeant and operating PX Cafés at airbases around the country.

When he returned from the war, my father opened a restaurant on the North Side at Argyle and Sheridan, and in 1962, opened Eli's Stage Delicatessen at 50 E. Oak Street. It was a great gathering place for the singles of that era, drawing entertainers from Rush Street including Bobby Short, Woody Allen, Shecky Greene, and Barbra Streisand.

My mother, Esther, worked with him all the years after they got married in 1948. I was born on the North Side in 1955 and grew up in the Edgewater neighborhood near the Edgewater Beach Hotel. You could really say that since 1962, when my dad opened the deli, my life has revolved around a few blocks in the North Michigan Avenue district.

My parents moved to Skokie when I was going into junior high school but later moved to Streeterville, and I have lived in Streeterville ever since. In December 1976, when I was a first-year student at Northwestern University Law School, I remember all of the alarms sounding in the neighborhood when Mayor Richard J. Daley died suddenly.

During the early days of our deli in 1962, there was no 1000 Lake Shore Drive, no One Mag Mile, the Hancock, or Water Tower Place. There were the nearby nightclubs like Mister Kelly's on Rush Street. Oak Street was a neighborhood street, and I remember Cassandra's, a dress store located next to our deli; the owners lived upstairs.

My dad, always a dreamer and a creator, wanted to be more than a "salami surgeon" and wanted to open a white tablecloth steakhouse. That opportunity came about in 1966 when he opened Eli's The Place For Steak in the then Carriage House Hotel at 215 E. Chicago Avenue. I was only 11 years old when it opened. My dad had both restaurants until 1968, when

Eli's Stage Delicatessen had a major fire.

The restaurants were always the center of my family life. I remember visiting the deli with my dad before my bar mitzvah in 1968 and then, after the party at the Drake, going to the steakhouse. I met my wife Maureen at Eli's The Place For Steak when I was a sophomore in college during one of the many summers that I worked for my dad. I even lived upstairs of Eli's for three years when I went to law school down the street.

After Eli's Stage Delicatessen closed, my dad focused all his time on Eli's The Place For Steak. My dad was the consummate host, and he wanted to greet all his guests personally—something you could not do with multiple restaurants. It was a different era back then, but the community was definitely a center of activity and energy that included the Playboy Club and people like Arnie Morton—just a fun place.

Eli's The Place For Steak was the place to go in Chicago in the 1960s and 1970s. We had many famous people who were always in the restaurant, including Irv Kupcinet, who would have lunch there several times a week, and George Dunne, who was there every Monday night. We continued on for a long time after my father died, and it was still "the place."

After graduating from Northwestern Law School, I practiced real estate and urban law at Arvey, Hodes, Costello & Burman from 1979 to 1984. From my dad, I gained a great interest in Chicago history. I have always been involved in groups that support Chicago architecture, including becoming a docent for the Chicago Architecture Foundation when I was in high school, serving as vice president and director for the Landmarks Preservation Council of Illinois, and as a trustee of the Illinois Historic Preservation Agency.

In 1984, I left the practice of law to join my dad to expand the sales of his signature cheesecake. The cheesecake had made its public debut on Michigan Avenue at the first Taste of Chicago on July 4, 1980. We are very proud that we have made Chicago famous for cheesecake, growing our business to become one of the largest specialty cheesecake bakers in the country and among Chicago's most famous foods.

My father died in May 1988, so I worked with my mother to operate Eli's The Place For Steak for 17 more years. It was in the summer of 2005 that we were forced to close when the building was torn down to become the new site of Children's Memorial Hospital.

After Eli died, his dear friends, including then Alderman Burt Natarus, County Board President George Dunne, and Bill Bartholomay of the Chicago Park District, honored him by naming the playground at Seneca Park, directly across the street from Eli's The Place For Steak for him. We chaired a campaign in the community that raised over $500,000 to rebuild Seneca Park and create the Eli M. Schulman Playground. We even had enough funds to purchase "Ben," an equine bronze sculpture by Deborah Butterfield. It was noted by George Dunne at the opening of the playground on May 7, 1990 that the equine sculpture was a perfect tribute as Eli loved horses and the racetrack.

Several years after the opening of Eli's Playground, I joined the Greater North Michigan Avenue Association, having found that my personal interests and career were oriented towards supporting its members and activities. My father had joined the GNMAA back in 1962. I have served as chairman of its board and continue to serve as a director and member of the Executive Committee. The role that I treasure most is as the founding chairman of The Magnificent Mile Lights Festival. We have hundreds of volunteers who work with the GNMAA staff and the city of Chicago year round to plan what has become one of the nation's biggest and best known holiday celebrations.

The greatest thing is when you come home at night and walk around the neighborhood—the restaurants, lectures at Northwestern, Lookingglass Theatre in the historic Water Tower Water Works, or the Museum of Contemporary Art. Another example of the area's diversity is The Clare at Water Tower, a major senior citizen project being developed in connection with Loyola University.

Although the restaurants have closed, Eli's still has a major role as institutional partner with the Greater North Michigan Avenue Association, and also in making sure that the Eli M. Schulman Playground and Seneca Park are maintained properly.

Michigan Avenue has a dynamic mix of residents, visitors, workers and students that vary widely by the time of the day, week and season. I see it as the ultimate urban community, and the cultural participation in the neighborhood really gives it many hues. For me, the fun of being involved in North Michigan Avenue is that it continues to be a street of restaurateurs, hoteliers, real estate developers and brokers and retailers, among others, all working for the good of the neighborhood.

The Pearson Street entrance to Seneca Park and the Eli M. Schulman Playground today (Eric Bronsky photo).

The Eli's Stage Delicatessen sign at 50 E. Oak Street salutes Chicago's new Roman Catholic Archbishop (courtesy of Marc Schulman).

The chefs and wait staff joined Eli and Esther Schulman for a group photo in front of their restaurant (courtesy of Marc Schulman).

Eugene Golub

In our company's early days, we realized that few people were concentrating their efforts on North Michigan Avenue. Personally, I think that Arthur Rubloff deserves much credit for developing Michigan Avenue, including naming it "The Magnificent Mile," and he clearly exhibited much foresight. Then, when Water Tower Place opened in the 1970s, it changed the whole character of the street and was a major move towards the future for North Michigan Avenue and probably the most significant thing that has happened in the area.

The John Hancock Center is an iconic property with a unique architectural style. It became a significant tourist attraction for both Chicagoans and visitors who wanted to view the city from the building's observation deck.

In the early 1960s, we purchased the International Harvester headquarters building at 180 N. Michigan when it became available after International Harvester moved to the then new Equitable Building. After International Harvester vacated the property we repositioned, remarketed and successfully leased the building.

We then acquired the building that was known as the Italian Court at the corner of Ontario Street and Michigan Avenue and built the now existing building known as 625 N. Michigan, which continues to be our corporate headquarters. During the same time period, we also acquired the 444 N. Michigan building where WIND-AM radio was a tenant. After the station moved to 625 N. Michigan, we demolished the existing building and constructed the new 444 N. Michigan. We also acquired the Blair Building at 645 N. Michigan in that period.

We never operated under a grand plan for which buildings we were going to acquire— we were just in the business of doing business! Although we concentrated our real estate focus on North Michigan Avenue and the Streeterville area, later on we expanded our interests and were involved in numerous real estate transactions all over the city and the United States. For the past twenty years we have also

been developing office and residential properties in Central and Eastern Europe.

The development process that has occurred on the Avenue required the tearing down of older buildings to construct new properties, which now include Water Tower Place, John Hancock Center, One Magnificent Mile, Neiman Marcus, and numerous other structures on North Michigan Avenue. Some have been renovated, like the Palmolive Building, and converted into top quality condominiums. We have seen an almost continual change and improvement of the area, including the new Conrad Hotel, The Shops at North Bridge, and 900 North Michigan. The historical Diana Court at the corner of Michigan Avenue and Ohio Street was developed into the Marriott Hotel.

In the 1970s we acquired five thousand apartments, which were part of the Lake Shore Management portfolio. Some of the properties in the portfolio were; 777 N. Michigan, the Ambassador House at 1325 State Parkway, 1150 Lake Shore Drive, and 3550, 3600, and 3950 Lake Shore Drive. All of the properties were eventually converted to condominiums.

Over the years the company has been involved in almost every type of real estate project, including complex, mixed-use properties. In 2007 we acquired the John Hancock Center and we are only the third owner of that important structure. The Hancock is a Chicago icon, and we have been successful in repositioning the office and retail space.

The street keeps getting better, and Mayor Richard M. Daley deserves much of the credit for ensuring that North Michigan Avenue continues to prosper. Residentially, North Michigan Avenue and the Streeterville areas have boomed and turned into high energy thriving neighborhoods. Rush Street and Oak Street continue to improve with high quality retail, restaurants and nightlife. Currently we are both an investor and on the development team for the new Elysian, which will add to the area because of the significant quality of the hotel and condominiums and its architecture.

Despite the current economic situation in the country, from a real estate perspective the long view is that Michigan Avenue and Streeterville with its wide range of quality infrastructure, is so well established that it will remain strong despite the fluctuating economic cycles.

Two views of North Michigan Avenue, photographed in the early and late 1960s, dramatically illustrate the metamorphosis of the avenue over less than a decade's time. The traditional architecture of the 1920s dominates this 1960 view from the top of the Prudential Building (photographer unknown, courtesy of the Chicago History Museum, composite of ICHi-25830/52291).

Later in the decade, developers were working in tandem with architects and civic groups to design a variety of office, hotel, and residential projects, based on architectural styles that were then in vogue (courtesy of GNMAA).

above

The Italian Court building epitomized the Burnham Plan and the "Upper Boul Mich" era. This building, which stood at the southeast corner of Ontario Street and Michigan Avenue, was created in 1920 by combining and modifying two existing apartment buildings (Chicago Photographs, courtesy of the Chicago History Museum, ICHi-52258).

right

Its most compelling feature was an interior courtyard that emulated a European-style arcade. This quiet oasis of urbanity succumbed to the wrecking crane in 1968 (courtesy of the Chicago Transit Authority).

left

A mélange of juxtaposed shapes and styles characterized Michigan Avenue architecture by the mid-1960s. In this view looking north towards Ohio Street, the modern glass and steel 645 N. Michigan Avenue building is partially hiding the Allerton Hotel. The 55-story 1000 N. Lake Shore Plaza building (in the distance directly behind the Water Tower) was completed in 1964 (photographer unknown, courtesy of the Chicago History Museum, ICHi-52300).

Lucien Lagrange

In 1959, I came to Canada from my home country of France. At the age of 18, I put myself through McGill University in Montreal, where I finally received a degree in architecture in 1972. During my third year at McGill, I remember meeting a group of architects, including Joe Fujikawa from Mies van der Rohe's office through the work I was doing as a draftsman (I was working part-time to support myself). Since I was already 27 years old, I decided that it was time for me to begin working in an architect's office.

So, I called Joe to see if he could help me find a job, and although they were booked up for intern positions at his company, Fujikawa offered to help me get a position at either C.F. Murphy or Skidmore Owings & Merrill (SOM) located in Chicago. I chose SOM and came to Chicago in May 1968. Since the SOM headquarters was located at 30 W. Monroe, it was a perfect place for me to get my first clear view of North Michigan Avenue.

At the time, the Hancock Building was still under construction. Although the Water Tower project had not begun and an empty lot still stood on that eventual site, one of the things that impressed me was a large mock-up that had been constructed on the site of a partial floor of Water Tower with an apartment in it. I remember that the display had windows of the potential view for tenants, and behind the windows was a photograph of what residents might see from the apartment. It was the first time I had ever seen such a mock-up of a residence, and I thought that was very clever because it provided interested parties with a future view of the lake and the city.

Among Skidmore, Owings, & Merrill's many projects in Chicago was the new John Hancock Building. Bruce Graham and Fazlur Kahn had led a team of architects in the design of what would become one of Chicago's iconic structures.

In fact, to my amazement, only two weeks after beginning employment at SOM, I was actually working directly with Graham and Kahn. I was in heaven because I was still a student at McGill, only a young man, and working with those great architects on the Hancock Building. It was also amazing luck to be working in Chicago during the summer of 1968 and located near the Conrad Hilton Hotel. It meant that I was right in the middle of the chaos that surrounded the events of the Democratic National Convention. One day during that infamous August, we heard over the office's loud speaker that the office was closing immediately and that we had better go directly home to avoid the violence taking place in the streets.

As I look back on 1968, I realize that North Michigan Avenue was very different than it is today. For example, the Marriott Hotel at Ohio and Michigan wasn't done, the Sears Tower hadn't gone up yet, and it seemed that there were few new buildings being constructed on the avenue north of the bridge. In fact, I can only recall such important structures as the Wrigley Building, Tribune Tower, original Water Tower, Drake Hotel, Palmolive Building, Westin Hotel, and the beginnings of the Hancock Building. The remainder of the street was predominantly a collection of older, smaller buildings.

Preliminary work had just begun on the site of the John Hancock Building in 1965. The building at far right, originally the Continental Hotel, is now the Westin Michigan Avenue. Fourth Presbyterian Church appears in the background (Glenn E. Dahlby photo, courtesy of the Chicago History Museum, ICHi-24065).

Watching the steelwork rise and knowing that the Hancock Building was to be the (then) world's tallest building gave Chicagoans a sense of excitement and anticipation during the late 1960s (courtesy of the Chicago Transit Authority).

Part 4
Monumental Grandeur
1970-1988

Two legendary Chicago landmarks, Water Tower and
Hancock Center, rose exactly one century apart. Each building
was an engineering marvel and was also the tallest structure
on the avenue upon completion (Eric Bronsky photo).

By the 1980s, the Drake Hotel and Palmolive Building, which have stood over the north entrance to Michigan Avenue like sturdy sentinels, were dwarfed by an army of much taller buildings (courtesy of GNMAA).

By 1970, new construction was effecting
a gradual but obvious change in the face
and character of North Michigan Avenue.
Scaffolding and barricades appeared on
several blocks, demolition crews moved
in, and successively taller or more massive
buildings soon rose to meet the sky.
This was surely a time of exuberance for
investors and developers, but also one
of genuine concern for urban planners,
preservationists, and residents.

The economic reality was an unprecedented demand for real estate along North Michigan Avenue. The old adage about the land beneath a building being worth more than the building was a frank irony in the case of several blocks of half-century-old buildings that had apparently outlived their usefulness. At least in theory, larger and more efficient buildings would generate more income, so property owners duly sought to replace aging structures with more profitable ones.

But the tradeoff here was variance from the Burnham Plan and the resulting loss of the intimate scale and historical flavor of the avenue. Architecturally significant buildings were razed, and initially some of the buildings that replaced them were comparatively boxy and bland—neither esthetically pleasing nor pedestrian-friendly. There was a certifiable fear that The Magnificent Mile would soon morph into a mere extension of the Loop with its canyons of glass and steel office towers jutting skyward from the sidewalks. The Illinois Center air-rights development of the early 1970s is an example of a project which, though financially viable, funnels pedestrian traffic inward through its warren of arcades and passageways while neglecting the streetscape.

But architects and urban planners do learn from experience, sometimes backtracking to correct errors and then applying knowledge gained to new projects. Designers were, for example, cognizant of the problems that would be generated by the extraordinary height and density of the John Hancock Building. Among other considerations, they set the tower far enough back from the roadway to allow for a sunken pedestrian plaza at its base and provided generous retail space.

Architecture continued to evolve; by the 1980s, buildings with setbacks, typically in the form of a wide base with a narrow tower, were de rigueur. An emerging mélange of different architectural styles leaned more towards Burnham's vision and away from the boxy towers of the '50s and '60s. The newer buildings were, in effect, a compromise between esthetic harmony and economic viability.

As high-rises continued to replace smaller buildings, civic leaders became increasingly concerned about the area's growing density. A proposed rapid transit distributor route, which was part of a much more comprehensive plan to improve mass transit in Chicago's central area, would have linked Streeterville to downtown through a subway running beneath Fairbanks Court. Due to opposition and a lack of funding, though, this project never progressed beyond the preliminary design stage. In more recent years, a proposed light-rail "Circulator" that would have served the River North and Streeterville areas met the same fate.

The advent of large-scale mixed-use developments combining retail, dining, entertainment, office, hotel, and residential units together in one complex began with Water Tower Place. Its almost-instant success upon completion in 1975 was undeniably a pivotal event in the recent history of North Michigan Avenue; it charted a new course and a much brighter future for the area.

Taste of Chicago, the brainchild of local restaurateur Arnie Morton, originated not in Grant Park but along a stretch of Michigan Avenue from Ohio Street to the river that was closed to traffic for just one day: July 4, 1980. Although this enormously successful event subsequently relocated to Columbus Drive, it paved the way for the avenue to host other special and seasonal events. The annual Magnificent Mile Lights Festival, sponsored by the Greater North Michigan Avenue Association, evolved into one of Chicago's premier holiday celebrations.

By the '80s, Michigan Avenue had eclipsed the Loop as Chicago's favorite place to stroll, shop, and dine. But as that decade drew to a close, the area's rapidly increasing density was creating some new challenges. Streets were gridlocked with traffic. Longtime tenants struggled to pay escalating rents, and the amount of vacant space became more visible. Some properties just off the avenue were neglected, and in some cases, blighted. Moreover, other up-and-coming Chicago neighborhoods were now competing with the avenue.

The future of the avenue's vitality and growth was in the hands of visionaries comprised of an erudite group of developers, business owners, and civic leaders. These individuals brought varying backgrounds and differing opinions to bear upon North Michigan Avenue, yet their expertise merged towards common viewpoints and sensible goals. Through their foresight and diligence, The Magnificent Mile would be kept on course.

As the construction boom of the '60s and '70s progressed along the avenue, a "canyon effect" was inevitable (courtesy of the Chicago Transit Authority).

Changes to the economic makeup of the avenue brought changes to its long-established retail tenants. In 1970, Bonwit Teller moved across the street to the then-new Hancock building, and the following year, the I. Magnin department store took over its old space. That store closed in 1992, and the building was then remodeled to house several national chains. Meanwhile, Bonwit Teller closed and was replaced by smaller specialty stores (courtesy of the Chicago Transit Authority).

"I tried to maintain a balance between high-rises, mid-rises, and low-rises, but I did not want to curb the 'economic engine.'" *Burton Natarus*

"The issue of height setbacks is important because you don't want to end up with a canyon effect on the street. And I think that's a real mistake because it means a lessening of the experience that people enjoy, which is light, flowers, and trees intermixed with people and interesting retail stores." *Peter Hanig*

James B. Klutznick

My father, Philip and my older brother, Tom started Urban Investment and Development Company in 1968. Before that, my father, an attorney, worked in government, serving as commissioner of the Federal Housing Authority under Presidents Roosevelt and Truman (he later served as ambassador to the Economic and Social Council of the United Nations under President Kennedy and Ambassador Stevenson, and secretary of commerce under President Carter). Commencing in the late 1940s, Dad created the development company that built the completely planned community of Park Forest, Illinois, where we moved in 1948.

I was born in Omaha, and we lived in Washington, D.C. before moving to Chicago in 1946. I grew up in Park Forest and graduated from Princeton University in 1965. While in school, I studied art and architecture, as well as urban and regional planning, but I ended up going into the Air Force in 1966. When I got out at the end of 1970, I went to work with my father and brother in the development business.

During the 1950s and '60s, Dad, and eventually Tom, built, among other developments, a number of shopping centers including Park Forest Plaza, Old Orchard, Oakbrook, and River Oaks. In those years, Marshall Field & Company was opening new stores in suburban shopping centers. So, my dad already had a relationship with Field's when they approached him in the late 1960s about developing a new store on Michigan Avenue. He negotiated the purchase of the land where Water Tower Place is today, starting with Sam Bronfman of Seagram's, who owned the front part of that site along Michigan Avenue where a Seagram's billboard stood advertising his liquors. But Urban Investment eventually acquired the entire block, including the old Pearson Hotel on the east end.

That is when I came into the business—in the early 1970s, when we started to build Water Tower Place. My initial responsibilities were to lease the retail and office components of the complex. Then, Maury Fisher and I formed a leasing and management division to service our own properties, particularly from the retail end.

While Water Tower Place was innovative, the concept of mixed-use goes back to the marketplaces and commerce of ancient times. The arcade buildings of the late nineteenth century and downtown Chicago's Auditorium Building were mixed-use. So, mixed-use is not a new idea, but one that has become more prevalent in recent years, particularly in urban areas where land values are high. It makes sense to promote multiple uses on a site to spread the cost of expensive land.

In a number of respects, mixed-use buildings may be more expensive to build than single-use buildings, but the sum of the whole is more valuable than the individual parts. This concept works particularly well in urban areas because people can do multiple things in a single trip. When retail, residential, hotel, office, and parking uses are combined under one roof, people who live in that building or from near and far have everything at their beck and call.

Having accumulated years of knowledge and experience in the shopping center industry, our company was able to assemble a team that understood how to design and integrate the various elements of a multilevel, mixed-use development. The architect for this project was Loebl Schlossman Bennett & Dart. They designed the building so that its retail and office mid-rise base fronted along Michigan Avenue with the hotel and condominium tower offset towards the east end. They did this to maintain the scale of the Michigan Avenue street wall concept. A number of buildings along the avenue have subsequently been designed this way.

The building is really a form-follows-function type of architecture. The retail component in the base, other than the entrances to the department stores, and the grand entrance to the shops are essentially inward-facing. The exterior walls of the retail base were not intended to have windows because service corridors run behind them to service the shops, whose fronts face the interior atrium and malls. The architect broke up the flat exterior wall surfaces by using multicolored marble panels, and created the arcaded walkways in the front and middle to make Water Tower Place more welcoming to pedestrians.

Initially, it was hard to sell Water Tower Place's vertical shopping mall concept to prospective retail tenants. Rather than a traditional street level storefront facing the sidewalk, they would instead be facing an interior atrium as much as eight stories above the street. When Water Tower Place opened in the fall of 1975, just the two major department stores were open for business. The atrium had to be open for safety and exiting purposes, even though all the other storefronts were still barricaded. It was a surrealistic but very interesting space that drew a lot of curious visitors because its general layout—the inviting street level entrance to the atrium, the glass elevators, and the rapid escalator system—was arranged to beckon people in and lead them up to the top level, both visually and physically.

By spring of the following year, approximately 30 stores were open and people just came in droves. The space was easier to lease after that. As you would guess, a lot of retailers wanted to be in the center of the lower floors, but it turned out that the top floor started to lease quickly because people tended to go up to the top first and then work their way down. It filled up over a three-year period.

Back then, there were not as many national store chains or specialty stores as you see today. A lot of the original retail stores were new concepts. We took a chance with start-ups and smaller chains. Some of them made it, some of them did not. But for savvy merchants, Water Tower Place turned out to be a very strong place to do business.

Retail merchandising trends change from year to year, and there is always turnover. American Girl Place is taking over a portion of the space vacated when Lord & Taylor moved out, and the remainder will eventually be leased. The economics of dividing that space among several tenants should more than make up for the loss of Lord & Taylor.

A key to Water Tower Place's success is that it was built on a large enough site to permit a physical layout conducive to creating comfortable and functional spaces. Vertical retail malls built on much smaller and cramped sites do not work as well, as the atriums are too high and straight-up. At Water Tower Place, your eye is drawn to other storefronts and walkways instead of just the atrium by itself because the atrium is lantern shaped in section, allowing views from level to level. This also makes vertical transportation more visible and accessible. You have to understand how the individual parts are interrelated—everything has to be coordinated and orchestrated to create an environment that people are comfortable in, is easy for them to navigate, and has enough variety of merchandise and services to make them want to be and stay there. Even then, not every aspect of Water Tower Place was successful. We had to make a few tweaks here and there, but we learned from our experience.

Water Tower Place remains today one of the best examples of mixed-use development in a major urban downtown. It broadened Michigan Avenue's appeal by opening the market to many more people. Previously, Michigan Avenue had been a relatively quiet street with a few well known specialty stores like Saks, Bonwit Teller and Korshak's, serving mainly an upper income clientele. But Water Tower Place, with its roughly one mile of retail frontage inside to match up with The Magnificent Mile outside, brought another approximately 100 stores onto the street. The wider range of merchandise and services appealed to more people with a broader range of incomes.

Michigan Avenue is deservedly recognized as one of the great shopping streets of the world. But back in the mid-1970s when Water Tower Place was getting underway, international stores were still hesitant to come to Middle America. They tested the waters in New York first because they perceived it to be more of an international city. Today, not only does Michigan Avenue draw internationally renowned stores, they have also spread down adjacent streets like Oak, Walton, and Rush.

A lot of this resulted from downtown becoming a more popular place to live, work, and play. The people who are moving into the Michigan Avenue area or visiting it have disposable income and will shop in those kinds of stores. It all works together—demographics, retail trends, and the growing desirability of Chicago.

The hotel and condominium tower portion of Water Tower Place was still rising in this April 1975 view from Harbor Point (Art Peterson photo, Peterson-Krambles Archive).

top left

When viewed from above, Water Tower Place appeared massive in relation to its surroundings until similar large projects were built nearby. Nowadays, it's harder to spot this building in current-day aerial photos showing a sea of skyscrapers! The mall and office space are contained in the building's two-square-block base (courtesy of GNMAA).

bottom left

The original Water Tower Theatres featured four screens. Located on the second floor of the mall, in the southeast quadrant, this space was later used for retail expansion (John McCarthy photo, courtesy of the Chicago History Museum, ICHi-52296).

top center

A 1975 view of the glassed-in atrium elevators, which were innovative for the time (Eric Bronsky photo).

top right

The main entrance to the mall in December 1975, was decorated with greenery and flowers. A cascading waterfall later replaced the planter boxes between the escalators, and then a more recent refurbishing brought an elaborate fountain with synchronized water jets (Eric Bronsky photo).

bottom right

Water Tower Place in 2008 (Eric Bronsky photo).

"Phil Klutznick, who developed Oakbrook and Old Orchard in the fifties and who was later responsible for building Water Tower Place, was a remarkable man. He had a spark in him, and anything that he did was the best." *Lawrence Pucci*

"I would argue that Water Tower Place is the most important factor in promoting the future development of Michigan Avenue." *Burton Natarus*

Burton Natarus

I was already alderman of the ward when the John Hancock Building opened, and I remember that Jerry Wolper was the one who began construction of that Chicago icon. However, despite being told that he was going to hit water during construction, he still started putting up the building. He wasn't able to finish the building, so he sold it to another developer who finished the job.

Another controversial project was the 900 N. Michigan Avenue Building on the west side of North Michigan Avenue. That structure is larger than originally anticipated because of the addition of the large garage on the west side of the vertical mall.

Back north, on the east side of the street, is the famous Water Tower Place that was constructed by Philip Klutznick. It was done without a planned development, and I fought the project because I thought that they should build the building's garage entrance on Pearson Street and have the exit on Chestnut Street. But they did exactly the opposite of my recommendation because they wanted to have an automobile pass-through. Now we are suffering for it because their argument was that they would have a tunnel pass-through, but last year, the new owners told us that they would have to close off the pass-through for security reasons.

North Michigan Avenue has certainly changed over the years because of intensified development and a subsequent increase in the density of the area. We have had some real issues over some of the buildings, like the McGraw-Hill Building, which they couldn't rent or sell. Our conclusion was to let John Buck tear it down and put up a new building on the site. There was a big hue and cry, but they ended up with a much better building [The Shops at North Bridge], one that is usable. He was also responsible for constructing a building at 600 N. Lake Shore Drive, between Ohio and Ontario.

Another important recent development is the Farwell Building. The city landmarked it and then passed an ordinance allowing them to take it down and rebuild it. The building was falling apart, and in exchange for all that work, the developer is going to offset his budgeting by building a high-rise to the north.

The avenue still has a combination of high-rise and some low-rise buildings. In the 1980s, there was a battle over an area at Chicago Avenue and Michigan, on either side of the building where Walgreens is located. The Reichman Brothers from Toronto came into Chicago to build [Olympia Centre] on that site. But there were some quaint little gardens and even a little observatory that were all torn down.

The stores located about two to three blocks to the south on North Michigan Avenue, on the same side of the street, have remained low-rise. They have been rehabbed, with different fronts on the buildings. We landmarked the very famous Allerton Hotel, where the Tip-Top-Tap used to be located and from where Don McNeill's Breakfast Club used to broadcast. Today, the hotel is still in business.

Redevelopment of the 900 N. Michigan Avenue property was inspired
by the unparalleled success of Water Tower Place. The previous building on
this site, shown in 1971, is best remembered for Jacques French Restaurant
and its inviting courtyard. Also fondly recalled are Tale of the Whale, a
seafood restaurant; and Sherlock's Home, a British-style pub (Betty Hulett
photo, courtesy of the Chicago History Museum, ICHi-24145).

This circa-1980 view of Michigan Avenue looking north towards
the Chicago River remains essentially unchanged some 28 years later
(courtesy of the Chicago Transit Authority).

"Ironically, despite a view that the street is very uniform in nature, architecturally, The Magnificent Mile is really a mish-mash. There are a great variety of buildings on the street, and yet, because there is a bit of everything, that is what makes North Michigan Avenue so great as compared with other great boulevards around the world. The street clearly has its own character."

Lucien Lagrange

Larry Levy

I grew up in St. Louis and attended Northwestern University as an undergraduate beginning in 1962. Although the North Michigan Avenue district didn't have much meaning to me when I was in college, one of my earliest memories of the street happened when I was going to the Kellogg School of Management for an MBA and drove into Chicago. I remember Mister Kelly's and the London House as well as going to Brittany Limited to buy my clothes.

After I received my undergraduate degree, I went into the army. When I returned to Chicago, I moved to 2801 N. Sheridan Road in 1967 in a Mies van der Rohe building and I was on North Michigan Avenue all the time. Then in 1975, I moved into an apartment in the Hancock Center. My impression was that North Michigan Avenue was an incredible place and the most exciting street I had ever been on, and I absolutely fell in love with the street.

Then, in 1976, Water Tower Place opened, and about six months before it was completed, I decided to build my first restaurant there. Although I had originally planned to invest in the restaurant business, I ended up opening up my own restaurant. I thought that what North Michigan Avenue needed was an old fashioned Jewish deli, and that Water Tower would be a place that would attract lots of traffic. The name of the deli was D.B. Kaplan's, and that was the first of five restaurants I opened, all in Water Tower Place. The building definitely developed slowly, and meanwhile, in 1979, I bought the land for One Magnificent Mile. That was my first high rise and downtown building in Chicago, and when that building was completed, our restaurant Spiaggia opened there about six months later.

Before I built One Magnificent Mile, my office was located in the building at Chestnut and Michigan, right across from the Fourth Presbyterian Church. H&M is located in the same place where FAO Schwarz was once located. Then we moved our offices to One Magnificent Mile, and I have been in the real estate business and the restaurant business since 1976. The center of it all was between Oak Street and Water Tower on Michigan Avenue. We haven't built any other buildings on Michigan Avenue.

I really enjoy the street and its wide variety of stores, hotels, and restaurants. There has been a tremendous increase in the number of prestigious residential properties located on or near North Michigan Avenue. In addition, many of the city's premier marketing, advertising, public relations, and other entrepreneurial businesses tend to have their offices on North Michigan Avenue.

I don't think that things are likely to change on North Michigan Avenue. Also, I don't expect that a lot of new Michigan Avenue buildings will come along since the avenue is pretty well built out. I have recently sold Levy Restaurants, but I am still very much involved in Chicago since I remain as the chairman of Levy Restaurants. I'm also involved in several major real estate projects in Chicago, Coral Gables, Florida, Seattle, Washington, and Denver, so I have enough to keep myself busy.

One Magnificent Mile, completed in 1983, combines office space with condominiums above. But the building is perhaps best known for the Levy's flagship restaurant, Spiaggia (Eric Bronsky photo).

A whimsical 1989 menu from D.B. Kaplan's in Water Tower Place featured caricatures of famous Chicagoans. Inside was a long list of sandwiches with names like "David Liverman," "Lox and Brentanos," and "One Magnificent Melt" (© The Levy Restaurants, Eric Bronsky Collection).

Christine Hefner

For a while, before my mom remarried,
I lived with her and my brother at
5801 N. Sheridan Road in the Edgewater
neighborhood, which was the only
high-rise on that entire stretch of North
Sheridan Road. At that time, the rest
of the buildings were older homes
that had been there for many years.

Then she remarried, and we moved to Wilmette. I would come downtown to see my dad at his offices at *Playboy*. I visited him before he moved into the Palmolive Building when the magazine's offices were on Ontario (not the very first office on Superior). They moved into the Ontario office in 1961, where the Museum of Contemporary Art was before they built their new building. During that time, North Michigan Avenue didn't have much of an impact on me because when my family came downtown it was to go to the theatre or a Blackhawks game.

After graduating high school, I interned at *Playboy* in the summer of 1970. Then, North Michigan Avenue was a mix of restaurants, boutiques, and office buildings. For example, I remember going to Jacques and Sherlock's Home restaurants for lunch. They were in the building that was torn down to build 900 N. Michigan Avenue. I also recall the original Oak Tree Restaurant and My Sister's Circus on Oak Street, a wonderful boutique located near the Esquire Theater. Many years later, my very first date with my husband-to-be, Billy Marovitz, was at the piano bar at La Tour, later torn down to build the new Park Hyatt Hotel. I remember when the Hancock Building was going up in the late '60s, as well as Water Tower Place in the early '70s.

I didn't go into the Playboy Club when I was a kid because you had to be 21 years old to be admitted, but when I was old enough, of course

I went. The Club was still in operation when I began working at *Playboy* in 1975, and, back then, every new group of employees at the magazine would be taken to the Club for lunch as part of their orientation. Of course, I would also visit our Playboy Resort in Lake Geneva, Wisconsin.

Then, one of the first projects I was asked to manage in the '70s was the development of a new retail concept called Playtique, which had been brought to the company by some outside retail experts. The idea was to combine two categories of merchandise on which young people spent most of their money: music and clothes. At the time, it was pre-CD days, so we focused on record albums, clothes, and accessories. We took over the first floor space at 919 N. Michigan Avenue that wrapped around the interior space where the Playboy Club was located at that time. Later, that became Mark Shale's. Now it's Louis Vuitton, St. John's Knits, and J. Mendel.

Playboy's headquarters remained at 919 N. Michigan until I moved them out in 1989. In 1965, the company had bought a 63-year lease-hold from Jerry Wexler. The company gutted the building and built some very distinctive and contemporary offices with curved walls rather than corners. They did a nice job with it, and we were there for more than 20 years.

We were still in the Michigan Avenue location when they started building Bloomingdale's and 900 N. Michigan. While the construction was happening, I remember somebody at the magazine saying to me, "Gosh, just when they are building a Bloomingdale's right across the street, we're moving." At the time, we looked out over the Drake Hotel on one side, and we would have looked out over the One Magnificent Mile building on the west side.

As for Michigan Avenue changing, as it developed south, that dovetailed with our move to our current location in Streeterville. I was certainly cognizant of the perception by some people that the "real" North Michigan Avenue seemed to begin at Chicago Avenue and go north to Oak Street. That was because that seemed to be where there was a concentration of stores and restaurants on those six to eight blocks. But that really changed as more was built from Chicago Avenue south to the river. So, when we came to our current location, we probably preceded some of the development of the River North restaurants, galleries, condos (six of which my husband, in partnership with the Cataldos, built), and the incredible expansion of Northwestern Memorial Hospital, but it was already clear that the area was developing. We never felt isolated in our location south of Chicago and east of North Michigan Avenue. I consider this to be a vibrant area that includes many beautiful apartments and condominiums even though it hasn't yet developed into what I would deem to be a commercial area as vibrant as west of Michigan Avenue.

below
The first Playboy Club opened in 1960 at 116 E. Walton, just west of Michigan Avenue. Later, the Club moved across the avenue to the Palmolive Building (courtesy of Playboy Enterprises).

right
Playboy was headquartered in the Palmolive Building from 1965 until 1989. During that era, the Lindbergh Beacon was popularly referred to as the "Bunny Beacon" (courtesy of Playboy Enterprises).

My family has had a shoe business in Chicago since 1944. When I was six or seven and we were living in Highland Park, my dad started taking me down to the store. By the time I was 11, I was cleaning and doing stock work on weekends. My dad was a terrific merchant. He really understood that you can't just open your doors and do business; he had a great eye for product and knew how to promote sales. The opening of one of our two stores on Diversey back in the early '50s featured Klieg lights and an appearance by Danny Thomas, a famous star at that time.

I worked my way through high school and college selling shoes. At Shimer College in western Illinois, my main interest was English and I decided that I was going to become an English teacher—I even have a certificate to teach in Illinois. But in 1971, there were no teaching jobs available, so I decided to join my family's shoe business full-time. For me, it was a natural transition. I learned from my dad, Irv, and my mother, Billie, who was an artist, about store design and shoe design. Besides selling shoes, I learned management and other aspects of the business. I thought this was going to be a short-term thing, but that was 37 years ago!

By the early '70s we had stores on Diversey, downtown at LaSalle and Madison, and the country's first Johnston & Murphy store in the Palmer House Hotel on Wabash. The downtown stores sold only men's shoes. We also had what is called a leased shoe department in the Turner Brothers clothing store in the old Sherman House Hotel. When the hotel was slated to be torn down to make way for the State of Illinois building, the Turner family moved their store to a one-story building at the northwest corner of Michigan and Superior, where Tiffany's is today. That was about 1974. We had a little four-seat shoe department there and ended up doing a tremendous amount of business. We met people from all over the country. It was an interesting, exciting, and fun time for us.

Michigan Avenue back then was certainly not what it is today. It was a lovely street, but I wouldn't say it was particularly exciting. Where Nike Town is today used to be a very nice Saks Fifth Avenue, which was a quiet carriage-trade store. Water Tower Place was brand new, and Bonwit Teller was across the street. Of course, the old 900 N. Michigan was a beautiful building that had a nice walk-through courtyard with Jacques French Restaurant, later Tale of the Whale.

And the Newberger family, who I'm still friends with, owned the old 700 N. Michigan building, which was a classic, stately building with retail on the base floor and offices above.

Unfortunately one of Turner Brothers' owners, Les Turner, died of Lou Gehrig's disease. Without Les there to operate the business, the family closed the store. I told my dad that we needed to open our own store on Michigan Avenue, and he gave me permission to look for a location. I walked up and down the street, wrote down the telephone number of every property manager on the avenue, and ended up talking to two parties.

At that time, the Marriott Hotel was being built on the site of the old Dunhill's store. We negotiated for a space in that building until we discovered that the ceiling height would be too low for our purposes. I then talked to the broker for the Farwell building, which had the former Peck & Peck store as a retail tenant. We negotiated to buy out that store's lease and then signed a long-term lease with the Farwell family, who then owned the building. My dad knew one of the Farwells, which helped in our negotiations.

Our flagship store at 660 N. Michigan opened in 1978. I would say that it was immediately successful. Originally we sold only men's shoes there, but so many women walked in asking, "Where are your women's shoes?"— and we did sell women's shoes in other stores—that finally, after about eight years, we added women's shoes. At the time it was a very tiny part of our business, but now it's the majority of our business because women like to buy shoes!

Today we operate five locations in the greater Chicago area, including our newest store in the John Hancock Center. This work has given me a tremendous opportunity for creativity, and I've used my teaching degree to teach people in our business. It's been a wonderful experience for me, one that I've enjoyed a great deal.

above

The Farwell Building, which has stood since 1927 at the northwest corner of Michigan Avenue and Erie Street, hosted Hanig's flagship footwear store from 1978 until the building closed in mid-2008 for redevelopment as the Ritz-Carlton Residences. Like the McGraw-Hill building, its landmarked façade will be carefully disassembled and then reconstructed as the outer shell of a new building (Eric Bronsky photo).

right

Relocated to the Hancock Center, Hanig's Footwear maintains its North Michigan Avenue presence as the last local independent retailer with a storefront on The Magnificent Mile, although technically, the store's entrance is around the corner on Chestnut Street (Eric Bronsky photo).

Bill Zwecker

We lived in the Lake View neighborhood until I was three years old. Then we moved to Oak Park, and I received my BA at Princeton University in American Civilization and American History. Back 'in the city, I applied for a bank training program (called The First Scholar Program) at the First National Bank. While it was an interesting experience, after about a year at the bank, I decided that banking and finance was not for me. So, there I was in my early 20s and I realized that I had to begin to decide what I wanted to do with my life. The answer turned out to be a fascinating career in journalism.

North Michigan Avenue has been a central part of my world since I was a kid. I have lived downtown ever since coming back to the city in the 1970s, and always in close proximity to Michigan Avenue including apartments or condominiums on Lake Shore Drive, Delaware Place, and in Streeterville. My mother, Peg Zwecker, was fashion editor at the *Chicago Sun-Times* and the *Chicago Daily News*. Because of her job, I was downtown on a regular basis while growing up, even though I was basically a suburban kid. However, because I had a working mother at a time when most mothers weren't working, a lot of my growing up experiences happened downtown. As a fashion editor, she focused much of her interest on stores all over downtown and North Michigan Avenue. Through her eyes, I watched the development of many of those businesses, and since she was very close friends with the famous developer Arthur Rubloff, the growth of The Magnificent Mile was something about which she reported.

At the Daily News, there were many famous journalists including Northwestern University graduate Lois Wille, who worked for my mother for a couple of years. In fact, Lois and my mother made a special bargain at the time my mother was looking to hire an assistant. Lois had no real interest in fashion and wanted to focus her writing career on urban issues. She had already been turned down for a job as a reporter, so she decided to apply for the position with mother who, after looking at Lois's writing clips, determined that she was overqualified for a job writing about fashion. Lois made the following offer: "Peg, I look at you as being an entrée to the paper, so I will propose a deal with you: I will be the best assistant you've

ever had and will give you two years. But, since I really want to get into the newsroom, I would like your support in becoming a reporter." Of course, mother was 100% supportive of that, and Lois and my mother remained good friends.

My dad, William Zwecker, was born in Austria. His family had been in the paper manufacturing business in Europe, but he immigrated to America in 1938 because of his anti-Nazi political activities. As a result, he lost everything, but fortunately, because of the family connections in the paper industry, Dad was able to obtain a visa and eventually get a job here. When he arrived in the United States, he soon became active with the OSS, the precursor to the CIA, because of his connections in Europe. He met my mother in Chicago during the war, fell in love, and they got married.

However, his work for the OSS meant that he was traveling back and forth to countries like Portugal, Switzerland, and Turkey. I regret that he was never really able to discuss his espionage work, and, sadly, he died before being able to write a book about what must have been amazing experiences. Dad focused on the specialty paper business and eventually used his knowledge to become a consultant to several paper companies. He was already 40 years old when I was born, and by that time, mother was a journalist. That was the world in which I grew up. My earliest memories of North Michigan Avenue are from that period, and I can recall coming downtown at the time when the John Hancock Building was just being completed in the late '60s and the tennis courts were still located behind the construction site. Stanley Korshak's store was on Michigan Avenue when it was the old 900 building, and Blum's Vogue was also located there (Mrs. Blum was a pal of my mother). I remember that when I later worked in banking I would see Mrs. Blum, and I secretly became aware that she was maintaining a checking account that contained $1 million. I thought that maybe the store was doing better business than I realized.

The other thing I remember very vividly was that my dad would repeat a story each time we walked past the Wrigley Building. He said that the structure had been the tallest building in Chicago when he first arrived here from Europe. That surprised me since, when I was a kid, the original Prudential Building was the tallest building. I remember going to the restaurant on the top of the Prudential Building as well as to the Tavern Club (which just recently closed) because my parents had a lot of family and friends who were members there.

Among the many famous places on or near North Michigan Avenue, I clearly remember the Cinema Theater on Chicago, just east of Michigan because of a special thing that happened there. While waiting in line for a movie, I met Walter Jacobson who, at the time, was a well-known personality at Channel 2. It was a thrill to see him in person. I also went to the Esquire Theater on a regular basis and recall that part of our routine was eating at Eli's Delicatessen on Oak Street for lunch, going to the Esquire, and then having dessert at an ice cream parlor near there or at the Drake Hotel drugstore, where we would have chicken salad for lunch followed by one of their wonderful sundaes.

Other than those places, North Michigan Avenue didn't have much significance to me. When I think back, I recall the development of Water Tower Place and going to Saks Fifth Avenue where, as a kid, my parents would buy my clothes. When I was in what I call my retail "period," I actually worked at Saks after I had my own store on Walton called Animal Accents.

I got into the retail business because I wasn't happy working at the bank and because some friends of my parents were in the wholesale manufacturers' rep gift business that was based at the Merchandise Mart.

My half-sister, Janet, who was older than me, was going through a divorce and was looking for something to do. So, my mother and I, in our infinite wisdom, suggested that Janet open a shop, and we offered to provide her financial backing to go into business. Mother, father, and I pooled some of our money and were able to talk Janet into the idea. It was during the late '70s, and at the time, everything in retailing seemed to be based on a theme, especially in kitchen and bath shops. I told her that since there were a lot of animal-themed products on the market, she should open a gift shop with a unique animal theme. People collected objects like that at the time and I thought it might be a good gimmick as a marketing tool. As a result, we opened the store. Thanks to my mother, we were successful because mother knew a lot of people and had an innate ability to get a lot of good press for the store. Our first location was at 56 E. Walton, across from what is now Bloomingdale's garage.

We opened Animal Accents in 1977 and were at that location from 1977 to 1983 before moving to the Hancock Building for another two years. One thing I learned by moving from a smaller space on Walton Street into the Hancock Building, next to the entrance to the Observatory, was that we needed to adapt our merchandise to the location. As a result, we became a quaint little gift, card, and tourist shop in the Hancock. It required a very different kind of marketing and merchandising.

During those years, there was a great deal of change going on up and down Michigan Avenue including the opening of Neiman Marcus as a direct competitor to Saks Fifth Avenue. When Tiffany and Elizabeth Arden's Red Door Salon opened on North Michigan Avenue, those stores signaled more changes on the street. I remember the time that Stanley Marcus came into our Animal Accents store and mother asked him to critique us and tell me what was good and what was bad since he was one of the great retail merchants in the world.

Overall, I think that North Michigan Avenue is considered to be one of the great avenues in the world, with a wide range of places to shop and merchandise to buy. In fact, when it comes to pure shopping, North Michigan Avenue has become a shopaholic's dream because you can find every type of product. And, if you are looking for the higher priced things to purchase, you can go to Oak Street and some of the other side streets like Walton where you can find those kinds of stores.

North Michigan Avenue looking south from Chicago Avenue, circa 1964. The 777 apartment building (far left), with a Walgreens store at its base, is the newest building in this view. To its right is the domed Michigan-Superior building (F.S. Dauwalter photo, courtesy of the Chicago History Museum, ICHi-38958).

The L-shaped Olympia Centre project, fronting on both Chicago and Michigan Avenues, replaced the old Michigan-Superior building with a bold new Neiman Marcus store conjoined to an office and condominium tower. The Allerton Hotel, now a landmark, still wears its illuminated "Tip-Top-Tap" sign (Eric Bronsky photo).

Part 5
Revitalization
1988–Present

The 700 N. Michigan Avenue building, a mixed-use project completed
in 1991, features the Chicago Place mall and a condominium tower.
Setting high-rise towers back from the avenue has helped to retain
a sense of openness (Eric Bronsky photo).

Efforts to make North Michigan Avenue more inviting to pedestrians
have succeeded remarkably well. The original sunken rectangular
plaza at John Hancock Center benefited from a dramatic makeover
during the 1990s. Kitty-corner from the Hancock, at the southwest
corner of Michigan Avenue and Chestnut Street is Plaza Escada.
This small retail center, designed by architect Lucien Lagrange,
is a nostalgic salute to the Beaux Arts style buildings of the
1920s (Eric Bronsky photo).

The more recent metamorphosis of Michigan Avenue is a process that has continued well into the new millennium. It commenced during the 1980s with the launch of several major mixed-use developments. In 1986, Olympia Centre built an L-shaped property with Neiman Marcus at its base and office space and condominiums in the tower above.

By 1988, new construction was in high gear. That year, the 1920s-era apartment building at 900 N. Michigan was razed and replaced by The 900 Shops, which opened in 1989.

Precipitated by the resounding success of Water Tower Place but designed to attract more luxurious stores and clientele, the new mall was anchored by the first Bloomingdale's Department Store in the Midwest. A setback tower rising high above the eight-story retail base accommodates the Four Seasons Hotel and The Residences at 900.

This highly successful project was followed by Crate & Barrel's stunning new flagship store in 1990. City Place, which opened in 1990 on the site of the old Woolworth's store, is an office building which also contains the Omni Hotel. The following year, a mixed-use project opened at 700 N. Michigan with a new vertical mall and the 100 East Huron condominiums. The mall, Chicago Place, was anchored by Henri Bendel and a brand new Saks Fifth Avenue, which moved from across the street. Though attractive, Chicago Place was notably less successful than other indoor malls at generating traffic, its chronic surfeit of vacant retail space serving as a reminder that careful planning and avoidance of past mistakes are crucial to the success of any urban project.

Meanwhile, south of the Chicago River, revitalization of the three-block stretch of North Michigan Avenue between Wacker Drive and Randolph Street had not yet begun in earnest. Apart from the redevelopment of the Union Carbide and Carbon Building as the Hard Rock Hotel, what should logically have become a grand connection between The Magnificent Mile and Millennium Park appeared to lack the elements that would stimulate pedestrian traffic.

As the older buildings that gave North Michigan Avenue its intimate character and scale were systematically replaced by towers of overwhelming size, developers and architects grappled with growing concerns that the massive new structures were choking out sunlight and greenery, making the avenue progressively less inviting. By the middle of the decade, with mounting public concern over such seemingly unchecked density growth, the Greater North Michigan Avenue Association was compelled to act. To address the challenge of planning for the future, a special committee within the association created a concept plan titled *Vision 2012* whose mission is "to ensure that The Magnificent Mile retains its character as a beautiful, vibrant, architecturally significant, economically thriving, and diverse community through the year 2012 and beyond."

Ralph Weber, *Vision 2012* committee chairman, reflected: "This document is now almost 11 years old and has served us well as a general guide. It focuses on three areas: activity and land use; urban design and scale; and traffic and transportation. The momentum for the area will include the continued construction of new buildings with many replacing older structures. At the same time, pressures for change and growth will continue. *Vision 2012* states that where new buildings replace older familiar buildings, our developers, owners, and architects should enhance the Michigan Avenue environment and experience with projects of high quality and design."

Clearly, *Vision 2012* was not a broad plan in the same sense as Burnham's of 1909, but rather a set of sensible guidelines focused on maintaining and enhancing the quality of the Greater North Michigan Avenue District. In particular, two major redevelopment projects that implemented *Vision 2012* philosophy demonstrate how economic development can achieve a balance with sociological, environmental, and aesthetic concerns. The first of these was 730 North Michigan Avenue. This block, bounded by Chicago Avenue, Michigan Avenue, Superior Street, and Rush Street, previously contained a hodgepodge of undistinguished low-rise structures that housed small businesses including banks and fast-food restaurants. The buildings were not demolished all at once but replaced in stages (a lesson perhaps learned from downtown Chicago's Block 37). The first stage, completed in 1997 and fronting along Michigan and Chicago Avenues, included low-rise retail buildings whose architecture emulates the classical style of the Upper Boul Mich era. The final stage, completed in 2001, featured the suave Peninsula Hotel with its entrance on Superior Street. To the casual observer, the various elements of this redeveloped block have the appearance of stand-alone buildings, yet they are actually components of one large, unified structure.

Equally innovative was the development of North Bridge, a nine-square-block retail and entertainment district encompassing new construction and adaptive reuse, thematically linked by plaques embedded in walkways and colorful fabric banners. The centerpiece of this district is the multilevel mall known as The Shops at North Bridge, anchored by a Nordstrom store. A portion of the mall occupies the site of the historic McGraw-Hill Building. Its original Art Deco façade was removed and then carefully reassembled around a brand new building whose upper floors house the Conrad Hotel. Another unique feature of the mall is that it bridges over both Grand Avenue and Rush Street. A nearby mixed-use retail and entertainment center at 600 N. Michigan, completed in 1996, is also a part of the North Bridge District.

Today's North Michigan Avenue does not quite adhere to the idealism of Burnham's Plan of Chicago or Rubloff's vision of The Magnificent Mile. Nonetheless, the avenue continues its long and exciting run as one of Chicago's most unique and successful neighborhoods, attracting new residents, tourists, and businesses in record numbers.

top right
In 1964, Charmet's Restaurant stood at the southwest corner of Michigan Avenue and Chicago Avenue. Next door, on Chicago Avenue, were Wimpy's and Old Cathay Cantonese Restaurant. The boarded-up building on the Michigan Avenue side would soon reopen as Le Garage Art Gallery (Sigmund J. Osty photo, courtesy of the Chicago History Museum, ICHi-18108).

bottom right
The entire block, an underused prime location, was redeveloped by the Thomas J. Klutznick Company into retail stores and the Peninsula Hotel. Today, Ralph Lauren's Chicago flagship with its tony RL Restaurant stands on the site of the old Charmet's (Eric Bronsky photo).

top left

The landmark façade of the old McGraw-Hill building, demolished in the late 1990s, was painstakingly reassembled around an entirely new structure housing The Shops at North Bridge and the Conrad Hotel. The main entrance to the Shops is a glass-walled structure located directly above Grand Avenue (Eric Bronsky photo).

bottom left

This view looks north along the main spine of the new North Bridge district from the intersection of Rush Street and Grand Avenue.
The focus of North Bridge is its collection of upscale restaurants, retail stores, and hotels (Eric Bronsky photo).

bottom right

Metal plaques embedded in the sidewalks at street intersections lend some identity to the district (Eric Bronsky photo).

Rick Roman

When I was a kid, we moved around a lot; we finally came to Chicago in 1968 when I was a preteen in junior high. The Democratic Convention was going on at the time, and I remember saying, "Dad, what kind of a place did you move us to? This place is unbelievably scary!" But my first impression of the city was the lakefront and Michigan Avenue, and I had never seen such an inspiring, gorgeous place. I remember shopping for shoes at Hanig's, having dinner at the Drake Hotel, and watching Franz Bentler and the Royal Strings perform. It was amazing. I was just totally enthralled with the downtown experience.

In my family there were firefighters, foundry men, a few teachers, and a couple of bar owners. I remember telling my dad I wanted to be in the bar business, and he said, "Oh my God, do anything but the bar business!" I had entered college at Marquette University to study biology, but transferred to the University of Wisconsin-Stout to get my degree in hotel and restaurant management. My first job was at the Hyatt Regency along the river; I worked for a few years at various food and beverage outlets including Stetson's Steak House and Truffles.

The John Hancock Building opened in 1970, and at the same time, a fine dining restaurant originally called The 95th was opened by Davre's, the fine dining division of ARA. Back then, companies that specialized in vending were not necessarily associated with fine dining, but one of ARA's founders, Davre Davidson, was a remarkable visionary who had the foresight to expand into a new area of business. Fine dining was just beginning to come of age within the restaurant industry, and so it was perfect timing for the restaurant to be built in a landmark building on Michigan Avenue.

ARA spent millions to build The 95th. Back then, it was unheard of for corporations to own such elaborate dining rooms and it was unusual for institutional food service companies to expand into many different areas, much less fine dining.

The original crystal chandeliers were a sight to behold. There were four of them, and they were enormous, 15 feet tall and almost 40 feet around. It would take almost two weeks to clean all four.

I was hired as the dining room manager in 1984. They were launching what was then called the New American Cuisine, which focused on the young, innovative chefs of the '80s who were reinventing American food. They needed to bring the service up to cutting edge and recruited me because they knew of my background with Hyatt. I was teamed up with Nick Pyknis, who had been the bar manager at The 95th since 1979, and we became great friends. Our job was to elevate the culinary reputation of the restaurant to a place of honor. At the time, a lot of rooftop restaurants had reputations for being touristy and ARA did not want that image. So, Nick was made the beverage manager, I was the dining room manager, and the rest is history; we've been here ever since...and we never get tired of the view!

Over the years we've gained a reputation for being one of the most romantic restaurants in Chicago—we love that part of our business. We went from being the wine place to being the romance place, a transition that we made during the '80s. When I first came here, the wine list was the big thing; it won *Wine Spectator's* Grand Award. We had 450 selections of wine and over

$1.5 million in inventory. Back in the mid-80s, that was a lot of wine. Our wine cellar used to be on the lower level, but now we keep everything upstairs. There was a theory that the slight movement of the building on windy days actually disturbed the sediment in the bottle—people talked about it everywhere we would go—but nobody ever returned a bottle because of it. ARA had a 20-year lease for the restaurant space which expired in 1990. They extended it for three years, but after that they wanted to close The 95th and relocate Nick and me to manage other venues around the country. Neither of us wanted to leave Chicago, so we decided to start our own company and bid to take over the contract for the restaurant. I still remember my boss's face when I told him of our plan. He said, "Are you crazy?" We went ahead, competing against some real heavies, and we were fortunate to win the contract. In 1993, The 95th became The Signature Room at the 95th.

We knew that attaining the stewardship of such an iconic place would be a terrific opportunity for us. A restaurant owned by Chicagoans, for Chicagoans. We wanted to pursue Davre Davidson's vision of world renown, and our goal has been to be recognized as a world leader in providing extraordinary food and beverage experiences. We're getting close; more and more people around the world are getting to know us.

You can't beat having The Magnificent Mile at your feet and Chicago further out; the avenue is a pretty special place. We've had the opportunity to serve some of Chicago's famous families including the Crowns, Armours, and Pritzkers; also mayors, aldermen, celebrities, movers and shakers from business, and heads of state from all over the world. It's been a remarkable experience and an honor.

The Signature Room has also appeared in films. Years ago, a Hollywood studio filmed a scene from *The Exorcist* here. But the highlight for us was when some scenes from the 2003 remake of The In-Laws were filmed here. They inquired about renting the restaurant, and we said that we could close it for an afternoon. They replied, "No, Rick, we need it for three weeks!" That was not possible! In the end, they recreated the restaurant interior from architectural drawings and photos on a sound stage in Toronto, and filmed only the must-dos on location. It looked so authentic that when people saw the movie, they didn't know that the restaurant scenes were not actually filmed here. We had a number of brides requesting the room that had the dance floor that rises from below.

I remember when I first came to Chicago I told my dad, "One of these days, I'm going to be on top of this town." And years later he reminded me of it: "Yeah, look at you, you're on the 95th, you're pretty close!" We laughed about that a lot!

The Signature Room at The 95th offers diners a view as sumptuous as the cuisine (Eric Bronsky photo).

A dizzying view of the John Hancock Center from the tranquility of the Fourth Presbyterian Church courtyard (Eric Bronsky photo).

Gordon Segal

When I was a kid, we did all our shopping on State Street either at Marshall Field's or Carson Pirie Scott & Co. I had an uncle who operated a little millinery hat factory in one of those industrial buildings off North Michigan Avenue, but I never really remember walking on the avenue until we went into retail in 1962.

From 1962 until 1965, our first Crate & Barrel store was in Old Town on Wells Street. In 1965, we built a new one next door, still on Wells Street. By 1976, we had converted our Wells Street location into an outlet store, and in 1980 we closed it and moved the outlet operation to North and Halsted.

By chance, in 1973, we had heard from Shale Baskin of Mark Shale about an available location for a new store at Michigan and Chestnut. Shale operated their men's clothing store in Joliet, but when he and his brother, Mark, decided to open in Chicago they named it Mark Shale. Shale was one of my great retail mentors, very bright and wonderful to talk to about retailing. We decided that the space at Michigan and Chestnut would be a good location for our business, began construction, and opened up in 1975. Even then, Water Tower Place had not been completed and John Hancock had been finished only a few years earlier. We stayed in that building until 1990.

I remember that during the 1960s and 1970s, North Michigan Avenue was an up-market street with a variety of wonderful little boutique stores mixed in with bigger, high-end stores like Saks Fifth Avenue and Bonwit Teller. I remember a wonderful little store called Anna's Flowers located in our building at Chestnut. In those days, there was relatively light foot traffic north of the river down to Oak since most people seemed to prefer to shop in the Loop, and the tourist business hadn't developed on North Michigan Avenue.

We had decided to move to Michigan and Chestnut because we sensed that the street was going to come alive at the opening of the Hancock Building and, especially, Water Tower Place. In fact, when we moved into our first Michigan Avenue location in 1975, I felt if we failed there we might be out of business, and I was concerned that the overall risk for us was considerable. However, the street had become very popular by late 1987, and for 15 years, the Crate & Barrel prospered at that location gaining both national and international exposure. Near the end of our lease at Michigan and Chestnut, our landlord told us that they wanted to tear down our building to erect a new building, and we had to find a new location for our store. So, in late1987- early 1988, we made the decision to buy the building situated on the southwest corner of Erie and Michigan.

At that time, there was very limited pedestrian traffic on that portion of North Michigan Avenue from the river to Erie, and it was strictly a concentration of office and medical buildings. I remember spending a year walking up and down the street and being seriously concerned that we wouldn't do enough business to be successful at this potentially new location. The concentration of foot traffic was north between Chicago Avenue and Oak Street.

When we started out thinking about the design for our new building at Michigan and Erie, our first inclination was to erect an office tower with our retail store located at the base of the building. However, the space had a very small "footprint" on the ground floor, and after going through many renditions of the building's design, we realized that if we put in a lobby and elevators and an exit for the office tower there wouldn't be much space for our retail business on the first floor. Eventually we made the decision to just construct our own smaller building at the new location and opened it in 1990. Today, it includes four stories of retail space, a partial fifth floor, and a basement. The building was designed by John Buenz of Solomon Cordwell Buenz, and it was great that John was a patient partner. We must have looked at 40 or 50 designs with him over a period of several months to come up with the final conceptual design.

When we were coming close to the opening of the building, one of the things we decided to do was design gardens that would be located in front of the store. My head of design, Raymond Arenson, said that he had heard of a young, new landscape designer who had just moved to Chicago from Peoria, named Doug Hoerr. Ray felt that we should talk to Hoerr because he might have some interesting ideas for the gardens. We soon came up with the idea of planting herbaceous and seasonal flowers and made the decision to change the gardens three times a year so that there would be tulips in the spring, wonderful summer flowers, and a series of fall flowers.

Then, one day in 1992, I received a call from Mayor Richard M. Daley's office requesting that I visit to talk to him about North Michigan Avenue and the landscaping of the street. Daley's idea was to put planters down the middle of North Michigan Avenue and plant trees and bushes. He asked me if I would undertake the development of such a plan. I thought about it a minute and said to him, "Mr. Mayor, I think putting planters down the middle of Michigan Avenue would be a great idea, but if you put trees and bushes there you would really be separating the street between the east side and the west side." I suggested that similar to what we had done in front of our store, we just use seasonal plantings down the middle of the street. That way, the street would stay unified. He agreed to that. His chief of staff at that time was Valerie Jarrett, who helped us inaugurate these planters in record time.

The landscaping idea was so successful since we started our plantings that the mayor decided to do the same thing between the river and Roosevelt Road. We worked with him on the design of those planters. The city also used Doug Hoerr as its landscape designer so there would be continuity from Oak Street to Roosevelt Road. I am very proud of it, and the mayor has liked it so much that he has also done similar plantings along numerous other boulevards like Congress Street, Ashland Boulevard, LaSalle Street, and Lake Shore Drive. I have since concluded that our mayor has a genetic obsession for horticulture and the greening of the city and that he realizes the importance of increasing the beauty of the city of Chicago.

The original Crate & Barrel store on Wells Street, circa 1962 (photographer unknown, courtesy of the Chicago History Museum, ICHi-32091).

Crate & Barrel's 1990 Chicago flagship lights up the southwest corner of Michigan Avenue and Erie Street (courtesy of Crate & Barrel).

"Gordon Segal is one of my heroes because he is such a brilliant merchant and has done so much for the city. While Gordy could have built a much taller building on that corner, he made the conscious decision to have architect John Buenz design a beautiful, relatively smaller building. Along with his gardens, that store adds to the ambience of North Michigan Avenue." *Bill Zwecker*

"North Michigan Avenue is a splendid mix of new and old. Crate & Barrel's welcoming dramatic illuminated interior beckons all passersby—a jewel unlike the more staid and tall buildings on the Avenue." *Ralph Weber*

Holly Agra

When I was 13, our family moved from the Detroit area to Cary, Illinois, and there I enjoyed a country lifestyle while my dad commuted to his job at American Airlines in downtown Chicago. One day, my humanities teacher took us downtown for a walking tour with the Chicago Architecture Foundation. I'll tell you, that was probably one of the first times I had ever been downtown. It's really remarkable that less than 10 years later I would be a major partner of the Architecture Foundation and operate a cruise line that provides some of their tours.

I had no idea that my first jobs would prove to be a training ground for my eventual career. I started at Great America when it opened in 1976, and then I worked at an advertising agency in the McGraw-Hill building at 520 N. Michigan. From my desk I had a view of the swimming pool of the Marriott Hotel, which was fairly new at the time. I remember thinking that I did not want to work inside the rest of my life!

My husband's grandfather was an immigrant from Portugal. He started the business that eventually became today's Mercury Skyline Cruiseline in the 1930s with a little speedboat that carried six people, offering rides from Navy Pier for 25 cents. Later, when he moved to Michigan Avenue, he had two 40-passenger boats. In 1956, he designed the Mercury, a bigger boat that would carry 110 people—that boat is still in our fleet today, renamed the Skyline Princess.

Before meeting my husband Bob, I had no real interest in boats; in fact I had never even been on a boat ride! We met in the wintertime, so I didn't even get to see his business until the first summer we were dating. My husband took over the business at age 18 after his parents passed away, so when we married, I walked right into a business that I knew nothing about.

When I began working at the boats, I had to find a place for myself because they wouldn't let me take over someone else's job. The elderly gentleman who had worked in the ticket office for both Bob's father and grandfather did not know me, and he was not about to let me touch the money! So I had to create my own job: I started a marketing department.

Up until then, this business had never really had much promotion. But having grown up in the world of travel, tourism, and hospitality through my dad's work for American Airlines, I just naturally used that background and inspiration towards sales and marketing while my husband concentrated on operations and Coast Guard regulations.

Our company grew over the 20 years that Bob and I divided the duties of the business. Inspired by people who operated businesses similar to ours across the country, we founded a national Passenger Vessel Association, offering many tools and contacts within a unique industry, and a short time later we decided to expand our business. In 1991, we launched our sister company, Chicago's First Lady Cruises, with different offerings than the Mercury sightseeing boats. Named by my mom, Chicago's First Lady now has two sister ships: Chicago's Little Lady and Chicago's Fair Lady.

To help fill our slow times and bring new customers down to the boats during the 1980s, I developed specialty cruises for our Mercury Sightseeing Boats. As an example, I invented the Wacky Pirate Cruise. This was on Saturday mornings, a fairly slow time for us. It featured a character called Buccaneer Bob and a theme song with kazoos, and the children would receive a certificate of survival. It encouraged people to bring small children and experience Chicago's waterways in a very fun way. Later, America's only Canine Cruise would evolve as one of our signature events.

Another special cruise that the company had always done was an 8 hour cruise of Chicago's waterways in the spring and fall. I put a marketing spin on it by giving it a name, The National Heritage Corridor Cruise, and offering it to the general public rather than just groups. None of these cruises would have been successful without our dedicated public relations specialist, Anita, who has helped us for over 25 years.

Early on, I realized that no one was going to visit my boat company without experiencing hotels, restaurants, and other attractions within the city. It made sense for me to be aligned with other associations that promoted tourism as their mission. So, for the past 25 years, I've been involved with the convention and tourism community, serving on various committees and helping to shape the promotion of Chicago. I was chairman of both the Greater North Michigan Avenue Association and the National Association of Passenger Vessel Owners. I also serve on the Executive Committee for the Chicago Convention and Tourism Bureau. And, in 2007, I became chairman of the Illinois Tourism Alliance, whose purpose is to remind state of Illinois legislators that tourism produces not only tax dollars but many valuable jobs around the state. Looking forward, all of these groups are excited about the possibility of Chicago hosting the world for the 2016 Olympics.

I also chair the GNMAA Away Committee. This is a small travel group that visits other urban retail and cultural destinations, explores what offerings they have, and analyzes what they do best in comparison to Chicago. We have visited eight different cities and right now we are contemplating a trip to Dubai! I feel that if the members of the business community on North Michigan Avenue want to observe the cutting edge of development and tourism, we really need to embark on a journey and see this unique destination.

Right now I'm involved with the city of Chicago as it begins to build and interconnect the long-planned river walk along the south bank of the Chicago River. Because our waterfront is two levels down from the street and sidewalk area, it has always been a challenge to encourage more people to stroll along the riverfront. Someday, the entire south bank of the Chicago River will be connected to the lakefront, and this will become a new destination in Chicago.

We feel that our company, as well as Wendella Sightseeing, have been "lone rangers" in promoting the river for the past 75 years, and now we would love to see the city and state join us in promoting the riverfront as a wonderful destination. It's certainly very conveniently located to Michigan Avenue, being situated between The Magnificent Mile and the Cultural Mile. Nearby Millennium Park has become a must-see destination. It brings a tear to my eye to think that we saw the opening of this amazing, wonderful facility, and it will continue to thrive for our grandchildren's grandchildren to enjoy. That will hold true for the Riverwalk as well, and we are excited to watch it unfold.

Passengers board Chicago's First Lady on the lower level of
East Wacker Drive, adjacent to Michigan Avenue Bridge.
In the background is the 333 N. Michigan Avenue building, with
Fannie May Candies on the first floor and Pucci directly above
(Eric Bronsky photo).

The Chicago Water Taxi and Ouilmette (background) belong to
Wendella, another local family-owned company that has operated
sightseeing boats for three generations (Eric Bronsky photo).

Peter Hanig

I brought *Cows on Parade* to Chicago, but I did not dream it up myself! In the summer of 1998, I went to Europe with my wife Alice and my son Daniel. We were in France and Switzerland on shoe business, and the last stop of our trip was in Zurich. That summer, Zurich was sponsoring an event called *Cow Parade*. They chose the cow because Switzerland has a large dairy industry and the cow is a national symbol. Upwards of 800 life-size fiberglass cows were spread throughout the city.

There seemed to be a cow sculpture on every tourist street. They were all very creative, and we took a lot of pictures. It was fun to watch other people's reactions to the cows—Americans would laugh out loud, and the Swiss would smile a nice little smile. It was a lot of fun, and we had a great time!

It was such a great experience that when I got home, I talked with several members of the Greater North Michigan Avenue Association, where I am a member, and we organized a meeting. With the support of the Swiss Consul, I obtained some photographic enlargements of the cows in Zurich. When I unveiled them at the meeting, everyone started laughing. A picture is worth a thousand words; they not only understood what I was talking about but also enjoyed it and agreed to create the same event on Michigan Avenue. So we organized ourselves and put together a delegation to meet with Lois Weisberg, who is still the commissioner of cultural affairs for the city of Chicago.

I had no idea what we were going to encounter. I had some books about the Zurich event, so I sent copies to both Lois and Maggie Daley, who I knew was involved in the arts. We met with Lois at the Cultural Center, and the room was filled with people. We ran through our presentation with posters and pictures, and I'm thinking, "Well, they'll send this to a committee, and it will languish for a year or two and maybe something will happen." But at the end of the presentation, Lois said, "Okay, we're going to go ahead and do it!" I was standing there dumbfounded, and she added, "...And you're in charge!" I said, "Well, I run a shoe business, " and she looked at me and replied, "You're in charge!"

My two wonderful co-chairs were Michael Christ of Tiffany and Co. and Daniel Nack of Salvatore Ferragamo, who used their many contacts to bring in sponsors. Both public and private sectors were involved. In just one week, Lois got a $100,000 grant from the Illinois Arts Council to get the project started. My wife asked me if I could afford to spend the time on this project. I said it would take 10 percent of my time. Well, it took 90 percent of my time! I would have nightmares about my house being filled with cows because I wouldn't be able to sell any of those things.

We put together an incredibly talented sales team because we had to sell this to sponsors. Lois was probably the strongest salesperson. She persuaded a group of large companies into participating. She's quite remarkable and has a great staff. The cost of each cow was in the area of $2,000-2,500 plus the artwork. This was to cover bringing the sculptures in from Switzerland, the bases, trucking, and other costs.

It was a slow start. We began all of this in October of '98 and our intent was to open by June 1999. And we did it! We had 330 cows, mostly in the downtown area but also in other parts of the city including the Field Museum, Museum of Science and Industry, and the gardens of The Art Institute. The response was beyond belief, beyond anything I expected. It was just a wonderful summer.

I really think that we were incredibly lucky. These sculptures were of Swiss cows, but cows tie into the history of Chicago—the myth of the Chicago Fire, the stockyards, Chicago being in the center of a farming community—so there's a connection. It's easy to turn these cow sculptures into dancers, movie stars, and other kinds of roles. People have an affinity for cows; they're non-threatening animals, and they give us many benefits. If we had picked something else, it might not have been as successful.

This cow, named "Visual Cacophony in 6 Mooovements,"
was the creation of artist Kermit Berg. Displayed on Michigan Avenue
just south of Chicago Avenue, it was plastered with photos taken at
CTA rapid transit stations (Graham Garfield photo).

Lucien Lagrange

My company has contributed to the growth of the avenue, both north and south, with such buildings as the Park Tower, which includes the Park Hyatt Hotel; and south of the river, the Hard Rock Hotel and the Blackstone Hotel.

In addition, I designed Plaza Escada, which we had originally planned as a vertical mall right across the street, with a hotel located on top. As we were progressing in our planning study, we discovered that there was a demand from a large retailer to be located on that site, in the 20,000 to 30,000 square feet of space. However, all of the potential companies demanded to be located at street level to have a North Michigan Avenue address. I would predict that there will probably never be another vertical mall built on The Magnificent Mile because of retailers' expectations for street level entrances, and, there has been a continual transition from the 1990s toward smaller stores located at street level. One specific example was Crate & Barrel. Gordon Segal chose the design of his building at Michigan and Erie to meet such expectations.

In the 1980s, Crate & Barrel was located at Chestnut and Michigan before moving to Erie. In fact, Bob Wislow of U.S. Equities was going to demolish that building at Chestnut and Michigan, erect the new Park Hyatt on the location along with a retail mall, and hopefully bring back Crate & Barrel. But Gordon opted for his new location and worked with John Benz as his architect to design a four-story building with Crate & Barrel as the only tenant.

My office continues to work on a wide variety of new projects, including the Elysian on the corner of Walton, State, and Rush. This is a 60-story building with 52 condos on top, a 182-room hotel below that, with the five lowest levels being used for meeting space, a Charlie Trotter restaurant, and some retail on the ground floor. That building is supposed to be finished around 2010. We are also working on the construction of the Ritz-Carlton residences and other projects around the city's downtown area.

I have seen and lived through the changes on the avenue with not only the changing real estate but the expansion of the hospital and the universities and the hotels. It is a multi-use location and quite complex, unlike LaSalle Street, which used to be just bankers and lawyers. Michigan Avenue is everything, and while Chicago is the center of the Midwest, the avenue is the center of the city and the Midwest for people to visit. The avenue is a very exciting place.

Water Tower Inn opened circa 1960 on Chicago Avenue just west of the namesake tower. It later became the Park Hyatt (courtesy of GNMAA).

In 2000, the dramatically taller Park Tower opened on the site of the old Water Tower Inn (Eric Bronsky photo).

Part 6
The Greater North Michigan Avenue District

A 1934 view of Streeterville south from Oak Street Beach shows the extent of early high-rise development adjacent to the north entrance to Michigan Avenue, creating a monumental gateway to the central part of the city. Generations of Chicagoans driving into the city on Lake Shore Drive have been mesmerized watching this row of prestigious buildings loom in the distance like a mountain range (Chicago Aerial Survey Co. photo, courtesy of the Chicago Transit Authority).

LAKE SHORE DRIVE

MICHIGAN AVE &
LAKE SHORE DRIVE

Streets and neighborhoods immediately adjacent to The Magnificent Mile have assumed a major supporting role throughout its history and growth, and share in its present-day prosperity. The immediately adjacent Streeterville and Rush Street areas, which existed before the avenue's creation in 1920, evolved with the avenue. River North, North Bridge, and River East are relatively new neighborhoods whose recent reclamation from pockets of urban neglect and decay may be directly attributed to the rise of The Magnificent Mile.

The Greater North Michigan Avenue Association recognizes the avenue as the core of a much larger district whose geographical boundaries extend south to Randolph Street, west to the Chicago River North Branch (but not Goose Island), north to North Avenue, and east to Lake Michigan. Further north and west, but included within the Greater North Michigan Avenue District, are the Gold Coast, Carl Sandburg Village, Old Town, and Cabrini-Green neighborhoods. These neighborhoods, too, share a fascinating history, but are less central to the development of North Michigan Avenue.

Streeterville

Various aspects of Chicago's history are inextricably associated with some of its storied residents. One of Chicago's most vibrant neighborhoods is named for Captain George Wellington Streeter, a Civil War veteran and rogue who for decades managed to elude legal authorities over homestead rights. Built on landfill jutting into Lake Michigan and typically defined as the area bounded by Michigan Avenue, Lake Michigan, and the Chicago River, a seldom-realized fact is that the east side of Rush Street is the true western boundary of Streeterville.

Taking into account its smaller than one square mile size, this area developed with a surprising breadth of mixed usage that goes back more than a century. Industries claimed the riverfront by the mid 1800s, and towards 1900, residential construction began to push onto the vacant land east of Pine Street and Lincoln Parkway. No sooner was Michigan Avenue Bridge completed than the neighborhood north of Chicago Avenue blossomed with impressive hotels and apartment buildings. South of Chicago Avenue, Northwestern University's sprawling medical school campus and hospital complex took root. Factories and warehouses, served by a branch of the Chicago & North Western Railway, mushroomed into the area between Ohio Street and the river. From the extreme southeast corner of Streeterville, the Chicago Municipal Pier, completed in 1916, extended into the lake. Of course, this popular recreational and entertainment destination ultimately evolved into the hugely successful icon known as Navy Pier.

Growth and development of the Streeterville neighborhood accelerated in tandem with the rise of The Magnificent Mile. The skyline became an architectural showcase for the works of Mies Van Der Rohe, Holabird & Root, and others. Its desirable and convenient central location attracted affluent residents with the promise of a new and exciting lifestyle. The university and medical campus flourished and expanded, currently boasting some of the finest and most prestigious facilities in the country. As property values soared, large parcels of land that had been vacant or used only as surface parking lots were eventually bought up and redeveloped.

The onetime industrial area located in the southeast part of Streeterville has undergone expansive redevelopment only within the past decade. This primarily residential area is so new, in fact, that its boundaries are not yet clearly defined, but it's popularly referred to as the River East neighborhood.

Though strained by growing population density and traffic congestion, Streeterville retains its dramatic lakefront vista, charming green spaces like Seneca Park, fine restaurants with sidewalk cafés, and some of Chicago's most noted tourist attractions including the John Hancock Center, Museum of Contemporary Art, and Navy Pier.

This is how Erie Street appeared in 1910, when much of Streeterville was still a marsh (*Chicago Daily News* photo, courtesy of the Chicago History Museum, DN-008119).

Captain George Streeter, reposing on a barrel by his "mobile" home, evidently had Chicago legislators over a barrel because their attempts to evict him from "his" land invariably failed (*Chicago Daily News* photo, courtesy of the Chicago History Museum, DN-008678).

Two photos of East Grand Avenue taken in 1915 show the drab warehouse and factory buildings of the post-fire era. Here, we're looking east from St. Clair Street. Bars and lunchrooms catered to area workers (courtesy of the Chicago History Museum, ICHi-16102).

The view west from Lake Shore Drive shows the undeveloped land at the east end of Grand Avenue. Note that the roadway in the foreground had not yet been paved (photographer unknown, courtesy of the Chicago History Museum, ICHi-38525).

left
After Pine Street, Lincoln Parkway, and Rush Street were fully built up, the landfill to the east became ripe for development. Ontario Street east of Lincoln Parkway was already lined with stately apartment buildings and townhouses before this 1915 photo (photographer unknown, courtesy of the Chicago History Museum, ICHi-8864).

By contrast, the south end of Streeterville, served by waterways and railroads, was heavily industrialized. In this 1935 view, construction of Lake Shore Drive Bridge is underway. Note that the North Pier Terminal building (beneath the General Electric sign) was originally several blocks in length. The massive Furniture Mart (center-right) also dominates. The Curtiss Candy Company, maker of Baby Ruth and Butterfinger bars, was a familiar sight to motorists along the old Lake Shore Drive S-curve (Chicago Aerial Survey Co. photo, courtesy of the Chicago Transit Authority).

Ralph Weber

I am a local product since I grew up in Skokie. I attended Northwestern University, majoring in mathematics, and enjoyed both living on campus and being close enough to family at home. My master's degree is in urban planning from Cornell University, and after graduate school, I joined Barton-Aschman Associates, an urban planning and engineering firm. After six years, I became director of planning at the Chicago Hospital Council before joining the administrative staff at Northwestern Memorial Hospital in 1980.

The campus of Northwestern University and Northwestern Memorial Hospital is located just east of North Michigan Avenue, and is part of the Streeterville community area of the City. There is a significant similarity between the growth of the campus and North Michigan Avenue, which co-exist in many mutually supportive dimensions.

My work at NMH has been a mix of planning, campus planning, and community relations. I have had several roles since coming to Northwestern Memorial Hospital in 1980, including positions as vice president for planning, campus planning, and currently, community relations. These job responsibilities have enabled me to be a direct witness to the dramatic changes in the area and on campus.

I have also served as liaison to the city of Chicago, the 42nd Ward Alderman's Office, and to the growing business and residential communities flanking the campus. In my role as liaison, my goal is to assure a good fit for our growing institution with the surrounding community. This involves good planning and good communication—never letting city officials or our neighbors be uninformed or surprised by our programs and projects. Considering their needs has always been an important part of our campus planning and communications.

NMH is the result of the 1972 consolidation of the Passavant Memorial Hospital and Wesley Memorial Hospital, both of which have nineteenth century origins in Chicago and which had relocated to the Northwestern University downtown campus in 1929 and 1941, respectively. Northwestern University located the medical school (now Feinberg School of Medicine) on the campus in 1924, and the campus also includes the NU Law School, NU's School of Continuing

Studies, and the Rehabilitation Institute of Chicago.

The campus is very dynamic. In the past 10 years alone, we have added three new buildings totaling over 3.5 million square feet. In 1999, NMH opened the new Feinberg/Galter Pavilion for inpatient and outpatient clinical care, followed in 2007 by the new Prentice Women's Hospital. During 1995, Northwestern University opened its new Robert H. Lurie Medical Research Building. In addition, planning is underway for the relocation of Children's Memorial Hospital from Lincoln Park, and it is expected to open in 2012 adjacent to Prentice. So, in a very real sense, the growth and the development of the campus are in sync with the past decade of investment in commercial and residential development in the area.

One of our biggest challenges for the campus is acquiring additional land for both the hospitals and university to grow. Over the years, we have acquired parcels incrementally and mostly adjacent to campus buildings. We were faced with an important opportunity about five years ago when the Department of Veterans Affairs in Washington, DC decided to sell its VA hospital located here. NMH was able to acquire this property, and planning is underway with the Rehabilitation Institute of Chicago for the development of future clinical facilities on the VA site.

Certainly, the construction of the John Hancock Building and the vertical malls have been the most significant changes on the avenue, but the areas east and west of the avenue have also experienced dramatic change. I remember the *Chicago Daily News* building on the site where the *Sun-Times* later took it over, and where Trump International Hotel & Tower is now being constructed.

As for Streeterville east of the avenue, in the late '70s and early '80s there was significant vacant property on land owned by the Chicago Dock and Canal Trust. The deeds for that property had originally been written by Abraham Lincoln and his law firm in the mid-1800s! I remember the Mandel Building in the early '80s, an industrial structure that was located at the river on the east side of Michigan Avenue behind the Tribune Tower. Few of us imagined that this and other areas surrounding downtown Chicago would experience the high rise residential boom that began in the late 1990s and continues today.

In the early 1990s, I and my colleagues at Northwestern Memorial Hospital began planning the Feinberg/Galter Building in order to consolidate and replace the clinical beds and services in the Wesley and Passavant Hospitals. Many health care experts judged our project as too big and bold. While we were planning in 1991 and 1992, the first Gulf War was underway and Hillary Clinton was proposing national health care insurance. HMOs were forecasting a reduction in hospitalization, and new technological breakthroughs presaged the conversion to outpatient care rather than in-hospital stays. We opened the new 2-million-square-foot hospital and physicians'

offices in May 1999, with 10 years of capacity for new growth. We achieved that growth in only 3½ years.

While we were determining the size of the Feinberg/Galter Building, none of the area planning agencies or utilities were projecting the residential boom that eventually happened. While some residential growth was expected, the amount was a surprise to many.

Luckily for us, former 42nd Ward Alderman Burton Natarus always supported this growth. But that was a friendship we had to continually earn and never take for granted. We knew that he was always watching the area on behalf of his constituents. He supported our case for new buildings and our plans to construct pedestrian bridges between our main buildings, which were necessary to connect technologies not replicated in our different care pavilions. Interestingly, you don't find such bridges in other parts of Michigan Avenue or in the downtown area, which were in his ward. We are now pleased to have established a good working relationship with Alderman Brendan Reilly, who succeeded Alderman Natarus in May 2007. Our hospital strives to be a special place, which is what being in the North Michigan Avenue area and the Streeterville community requires.

The Northwestern University Medical School campus along East Superior Street was under construction in 1926 (*Chicago Daily News* photo, courtesy of the Chicago History Museum, DN-0082418).

A current-day view of NMH's Feinberg (foreground) and Galter Pavilions on east Erie Street between Fairbanks Court and St. Clair Street (Eric Bronsky photo).

Enclosed pedestrian bridges over the intersection of Fairbanks Court and Huron Street connect the Feinberg Pavilion (left) with the Olson Pavilion (center) and the Lurie Medical Research Center (right) (Eric Bronsky photo).

Burton Natarus

It was quite an undertaking to develop the Northwestern Memorial Hospital portion of the Streeterville neighborhood. It seems that many of the physicians from the two hospitals that were in operation there did not talk to each other. One man who was key in developing NMH was David Everhart; he was able to get the doctors of Passavant talking to the doctors of Wesley. Then, Dolly and Jack Galter gave money for the construction of Galter Pavilion, and Reuben Feinberg did the same thing for the Feinberg Pavilion.

Another key development happened when Henry Betts decided to raise money and build a new structure that became the Rehabilitation Institute of Chicago. The Rehab Institute is now part of Northwestern Memorial Hospital. Abra Prentice Wilkin was yet another key contributor in the development of the hospital complex. Her charitable foundation donated much of the funds to build the new Prentice Women's Hospital.

At one point, Northwestern Memorial Hospital decided to sell some of the land they owned and build four high-rise buildings on the north side of Pearson Street. We had a big fight over that because people didn't want any tall buildings there.

The other big controversy happened when they decided to close the VA Hospital. Northwestern Memorial won the bid to buy that building and continue providing medical services to veterans. Northwestern University worked together with the neighborhood to build a big research center, and they gained huge government grants to conduct medical research. Of course, the Northwestern Medical School is located there as well as the Northwestern Law School, to which Arthur Rubloff had donated a lot of money for their continued operation. The American Bar Association and the American Dental Association also have their headquarters in the neighborhood.

To the south of the hospital was a huge National Guard Armory. At the time it was built, it was very fashionable to have National Guard armories located within the city where the U.S. military would conduct training. The city relied on it in 1968 during the riots brought on after the Dr. Martin Luther King assassination—there

was great turmoil across the West and Near North Sides. That same year there were riots around the Democratic National Convention at the Amphitheater as well as gang problems at Cabrini-Green. Some National Guardsmen were stationed at the armory to help during those troubling times. Later, the government decided to sell the armory because it was old and decaying. After they tore down the armory, the Museum of Contemporary Art built a new museum on that site.

The Streeterville neighborhood includes many buildings that were erected as early as the 1920s. At 180 E. Pearson was the Pearson Hotel that was torn down to make room for Water Tower Place. The Mies Van der Rohe buildings, constructed on East Lake Shore Drive, took us 10 years to gain landmark status. They blamed me for the delay, but they were wrong. There was one board of directors that fought the designation. As long as there was one group against it, we couldn't landmark them, but the buildings finally did receive landmark status.

I was clearly responsible for gaining landmark status for many buildings in my ward and around the entire downtown area, but that has also meant that some of my critics have accused me of being closely involved with developers. That isn't true because I have designated many different sized buildings as landmarks, and developed and saved more brownstones and low-rise housing than anybody else in the city. I tried to maintain a balance between high-rises, mid-rises, and low-rises, but I did not want to curb the "economic engine." We wrote all the environmental "green belt incentives" into the city's zoning code when I was on the Mayor's Zoning Reform Commission.

top left

It wasn't until approximately two decades after World War II that the construction boom progressed eastward of Michigan Avenue. This view shows Chestnut Street, looking west from DeWitt Place, before the John Hancock Building and Water Tower Place were constructed (Harry Williams photo, courtesy of the Chicago Transit Authority).

top right

A 1936 aerial view of Streeterville shows a substantial amount of undeveloped acreage. Lake Shore Drive appears in the foreground, and the intersecting streets are (left to right) Chicago Avenue, Pearson Street, and Chestnut Street. The National Guard Armory is prominent in the center. The Water Tower is visible in the background, and NU Medical School is on the left (108th Photo Section, courtesy of the Chicago History Museum, ICHi-19697).

bottom right

A more recent view of Streeterville's dramatic skyline centers on Chicago Avenue (courtesy of the Chicago Transit Authority).

Eugene Golub

Since the 1960s, we have been in the
business of acquiring, developing,
repositioning, and marketing real estate,
with a heavy concentration on the Greater
North Michigan Avenue area. In the late
'80s, we acquired 680 North Lake Shore
Drive, which was originally the Furniture
Mart. We purchased the building out
of bankruptcy and successfully repositioned
the property. The structure is the
largest adaptive re-use building in the
United States that has condominiums,
retail, office space. and parking.

Some of the premier tenants of the 680 building are Playboy Enterprises, Northwestern Memorial Faculty Foundation, Northwestern University Medical School and the Northwestern Orthopedic Institutue.

We recently completed the 50 story Streeter residential rental tower and the second phase, Streeter Place, is under construction. Golub & Company also owns the CBS Channel 2 site at the corner of Erie Street and McClurg Court. CBS has moved its studios to Block 37, where we have completed the 22 W. Washington office building anchored by CBS and Morningstar.

A few years ago, we acquired the Time-Life building at 541 Fairbanks Court. At the corners of Rush and Delaware we built the Bristol Condominiums and converted the 40 E. Delaware building to condominiums.

The southeast quadrant of Streeterville was still a sea of surface parking lots at the time of this aerial photo in 1968, but one sure sign of forthcoming change was the newly completed Lake Point Tower (upper-left). Later converted to condominiums, it was for awhile the tallest apartment building in the world. Outer Drive East, now 400 E.

Randolph Condominiums (upper-right), had been completed in 1963. The success of these two pioneering residential developments and the eventual sale of vacant land owned by the Chicago Dock & Canal Trust ultimately helped to spur the current building boom centered in the River East portion of Streeterville (courtesy of GNMAA).

Gail Spreen

I grew up in Medford, Wisconsin, 3½ hours north of Madison, in a large family. Looking back, I realize that I probably knew everyone in my home town and I realize that the concept of "community" has always been important to me. I received an undergraduate degree at UW-Eau Claire in music education and, after graduation, taught instrumental music to students in grades six through twelve. However, after three years of teaching, I found the work unfulfilling.

As a result of that conclusion, I made the decision to leave the teaching profession and move to Aspen, Colorado where I ended up living for four years. They have a famous music festival in Aspen every year, and it became a part of my life. Since I also loved to ski, Colorado was a perfect fit at that point in my life. I must admit that I had a wonderful time there in the late '80s and really got to know many people in the town.

However, after a few years passed in Aspen, I realized that I rarely read a newspaper or a book and knew almost nothing about the news of the day because I had become so engrossed in my new world of fun and fantasy. That conclusion led to the decision to return to the Midwest and get serious again. I settled in Chicago in 1989 rather than return to Wisconsin and began my career in real estate with Draper and Kramer. I worked for them for seven years in commercial mortgage and appraising before shifting to asset management and managing condo conversions. After realizing my love for real estate work, I was able to earn my sales, brokerage, and appraisers licenses, and did all that while continuing to work for Draper and Kramer.

In 1997, I joined MCL Companies in Streeterville. After they bought all of Chicago Dock & Canal's interest in this area, the first thing they wanted to do was condo conversions and new construction. MCL converted 440 and 480 N. McClurg into condominiums from rental properties. I was the project manager for those buildings, and since 1997, have found myself directly in the middle of all the ongoing activities in the Streeterville neighborhood.

After focusing on new construction projects, I shifted my time towards opening Streeterville Properties and getting active in the community through SOAR (Streeterville Organization for Active Residents). Our primary mission at SOAR is to work on behalf of the residents of Streeterville by preserving, promoting, and enhancing the quality of their lives in the community. We work hard to build the feeling of "neighborhood" in the area. SOAR has been around for 33 years, since 1975, so it is not a single-topic organization.

Despite some complaints, we at SOAR are definitely not anti-development—we know that things are going to be built, and we think that this is the greatest neighborhood in the city. Our challenge is how to continue development and growth and still keep a balance of uses. We work with numerous developers, which is nice because some of the best developers in the city are working in Streeterville. We have the opportunity to review their projects, make recommendations, and actually see a lot of those suggestions being implemented.

It has been a phenomenal time of change for the Streeterville area, which has become the center of a building boom. Since 1997, nearly all of the surface parking lots have been replaced with new construction or new parks. We seek to differentiate ourselves from other neighborhoods where a lot of new high rises aren't necessarily the best designs. If any of our unobstructed views is going to be lost, it should be replaced with great, architecturally significant buildings.

SOAR tries to encourage developers and architects to bring us only the absolute best designs and projects. A good example is the Chicago Spire, which is now under construction at the east end of East North Water Street next to Ogden Slip. On the south parcel of land along the river will be a plaza with sculpture and an open area.

Santiago Calatrava, the architect of the Spire, is also an artist who thinks in multi-dimensional levels. Two different versions of the Spire had been proposed through the years. The first one, by the Fordham Company and Chris Carley, received our support. A lot of people were surprised that SOAR was in favor of a project that was going to be 2,000 feet tall in this neighborhood. But we thought it was very elegant, something that would add to the neighborhood.

However, Fordham lost the land to Kelleher and Shelbourne Development. Thankfully, Shelbourne wanted to go down the same path and work with Calatrava. They changed the Fordham Company's first design for the building and made it all condominiums instead of hotels and condos. The new proposal called for a wider girth all the way around the building with an underground garage. We considered that approach to be a plus for the neighborhood.

The Fordham Company has bought another lot just to the west, in front of the Sheraton Hotel, and is now proposing an 1,100-foot-tall building. It's almost as tall as the Hancock, and they are calling it the "Spire's Little Brother" because it's also glass and kind of has a turn/twist to it. Called the Waldorf-Astoria, it will be half condos and half hotel rooms. It's in the final stages of approval.

MCL was the primary developer of the area when they bought all this land from Chicago Dock & Canal. But now, I think we have 10 different developers doing whatever they want without a coordinated plan of action, and that has created a challenge for SOAR and the neighborhood. However, that is changing thanks to SOAR's new initiative called "The Big Picture in South Streeterville." We recently had a meeting to discuss the challenges and hear the opinions of people representing several local business and civic groups. We who are here all the time, in the middle of all this construction, realize that we might become jaded and not see the larger picture.

One of the geographic factors in our favor is that we have water on three sides of the neighborhood. We should be bringing "water" into our streetscape, softening it, going greener, and maybe become more of an eco-friendly neighborhood than any other area. We do have several parks in operation or planned for the neighborhood including DuSable Park east of the Spire, Ogden Plaza in front of the Sheraton Hotel, which is going to be redone, and a park between the Waldorf-Astoria and a new building across from the AMC theaters. We encourage building more little parks where residents and visitors can take a moment to relax during the day.

The availability of attractive hotel space is another goal. In fact, several of the proposed condominium buildings in Streeterville have now switched to become hotels. The Waldorf-Astoria will be a high-end hotel and the Sheraton, Embassy Suites, and W Hotel are all located within Streeterville.

As for grocery shopping, we are pretty well supplied with stores like Fox & Obel, Dominick's, and Treasure Island; and we have more restaurants coming in all the time. In addition, some spas, nail salons, and other services are opening up in Streeterville. One problem continues to be the proliferation of banks throughout the neighborhood that do not create any kind of character or particular appeal. Ironically, I have been told by some of the banks that Streeterville's demographics are great for that kind of business.

The Streeterville Chamber of Commerce has a tag line called, "The Complete Package. We Have Everything Here: From the institutions, to museums, to the lakefront, to absolutely everything available." We strongly feel that Streeterville is going to be the hot area in coming years, comparable to Manhattan but hopefully better, friendlier, greener, and soft and inviting.

Al's Fishery at 416 E. Grand Avenue was just a short stroll from Navy Pier. This longtime Streeterville institution harked back to an era when commercial fisheries were common to Chicago's lakefront neighborhoods. The delectable fried shrimp and witty proprietor always attracted a lunchtime crowd. Al's closed in 1986 (John McCarthy photo, courtesy of the Chicago History Museum, ICHi-52264).

The portion of Streeterville just east of Michigan Avenue has evolved with the avenue. In this 1968 photo, art galleries, boutiques, and hotels line the north side of Ontario Street just east of Michigan. Today, a sleek glass tower with an Orvis store specializing in fly fishing gear occupies the site of the old limestone façade in the foreground. Sears Vincent Price Gallery of Fine Art is now Burberry Ltd. (Sigmund J. Osty photo, courtesy of the Chicago History Museum, ICHi-52280).

The Museum of Contemporary Art opened at 237 E. Ontario Street in 1967. Enormously popular and successful, the museum expanded in 1979 but eventually outgrew its original location and moved to a spacious new facility on the site of the old National Guard Armory in 1996. The Holiday Inn and Time-Life Building are visible in the background (courtesy of the Chicago Transit Authority).

Rush and Oak Streets

Rush Street, situated just one block west and running more or less parallel to Michigan Avenue, predated the avenue by approximately 80 years. For much of the nineteenth century, Rush reigned as the easternmost thoroughfare connecting downtown with the Near North Side. Regarded, too, as one of Chicago's most desirable residential streets, it was lined with mansions and small hotels well into the twentieth century.

The widening of Pine Street and the completion of Michigan Avenue Bridge attracted commercial development, creating a demand for Rush Street property. Restaurants and nightclubs desiring a prestigious Magnificent Mile location but thwarted by rising rents viewed the adjacent Rush Street as an affordable alternative. During the postwar years, Rush emerged as a premier dining and entertainment district second only to Randolph Street. The annual Gold Coast Art Fair (since relocated to the River North neighborhood) attracted throngs of people. Although the peak years of the '60s were followed by two decades of stagnation and decline, the entire stretch later rebounded as an upscale residential neighborhood lined with brand new condominiums, hotels, boutiques, fine restaurants, and popular bars.

Of course, the manifold successes of Michigan Avenue and Rush Street overflowed onto the side streets that connect both thoroughfares. Shoehorned into a one-block stretch of Oak Street linking Rush to The Magnificent Mile, Oak Street Beach, and East Lake Shore Drive is an amazing collection of late nineteenth century graystone residences which today house luxury boutiques and salons. New low-rise buildings replaced a few of the old mansions through the years, but otherwise, this block's historical character and intimate scale remain remarkably intact. In fact, today's Oak Street is reminiscent of how Michigan Avenue looked in its heyday.

top left
Today's Rush Street is vastly changed from its nineteenth and early twentieth century usage and appearance. In this 1916 view looking north from Rush Street Bridge, autos approaching the bridge bump across the C&NW tracks at North Water Street. The blocks between the river and Grand Avenue were filled primarily with factories and warehouses (Eric Bronsky Collection).

bottom left
Rush Street, looking south from Chicago Avenue in 1915.
As affluent residents migrated to fashionable neighborhoods further north, the street began to look rather bleak (photographer unknown, courtesy of the Chicago History Museum, ICHi-14150).

top right
Rush Street, looking north from Grand Avenue in 1915.
Two blocks of small hotels and neighborhood businesses between Grand and Ontario Street served as a buffer between the riverfront industries and the mansions just to the north (photographer unknown, courtesy of the Chicago History Museum, ICHi-04681).

bottom right
By the early 1920s, construction cranes and structural steel framework on nearby North Michigan Avenue were beginning to cast a shadow over Rush Street. This view looks northeast from Rush and Pearson Street. The rising framework in the middle of the photo is the Central Life Insurance Co. Building (courtesy of GNMAA).

above

As land values skyrocketed and upkeep became unaffordable, nearly all of Rush Street's legendary mansions followed the inevitable pathway from splendor to neglect to oblivion. In the period following the Great Fire, a portion of Rush Street was adopted by several members of the McCormick family as the site for some of Chicago's splendid mansions. The Cyrus McCormick residence and its landscaped grounds, shown circa 1900, occupied the east side of Rush between Erie Street and Huron Street (photographer unknown, courtesy of the Chicago History Museum, CRC-133C).

top right

By 1923, the brand new Central Life Insurance Co. Building and the Allerton Hotel loomed over the residence (photographer unknown, courtesy of the Chicago History Museum, ICHi-52304).

bottom right

The house stood vacant after World War II, and by 1950, the sign posted in front of the by then dilapidated building read, "Prestige location for sale, lease or development" (Dr. Frank E. Rice photo, courtesy of the Chicago History Museum, ICHi-19736).

"Rush Street was always where the action was, including Mister Kelly's for performances of Streisand, Midler and others. We'd cover these shows as news reporters and didn't have to pay, but left tips for the bartenders. Our rival, *Sun-Times* columnist Irv Kupcinet, usually fell asleep and rarely left anything! Later in the disco years, Faces was the hot spot. O'Connell's' was the hamburger spot of choice and the Cinema Theater had more sophisticated and often foreign films, as did the Surf on Chicago Avenue." *Abra Prentice Wilkin*

North of Chicago Avenue, the stretch of Rush Street that ran on a northwesterly angle to Cedar Street was Chicago's longtime nightclub district. This 1956 bird's-eye view looks north from Chestnut Street (photographer unknown, courtesy of the Chicago History Museum, ICHi-51690).

Rush Street's concentration of restaurants and bars featured live jazz, comedy, and burlesque. The district was in its prime when this 1963 photo looking north from Walton Street was taken (Sigmund J. Osty photo, courtesy of the Chicago History Museum, ICHi-52284).

Rush Street always came alive after dark. This view looks south from Bellevue Place in the summer of 1959 during the Gold Coast Art Fair (Marty Schmidt photo, courtesy of the Chicago History Museum, ICHi-51458).

Burton Natarus

I came to Chicago from Wausau, Wisconsin in 1960 and became alderman of the 42nd Ward in 1971. In the 1960s, I lived on Rush Street in a brownstone above Gus's Pub with a bunch of bachelors. We were across the street from Gibson's, which was at that time the famous Mister Kelly's, a popular nightclub where such stars as Frank Sinatra used to perform.

To the north was Adolph's Italian Restaurant, Larry's All-Night Bar, and the coffee shop, O'Connell's. That was where I met my wife, and we were married for 28 years. At State and Bellevue, the Newberry Library was situated near what became Mariano Park, named after Lou Mariano, the co-editor of the *Encyclopedia Britannica*, who would sit in the window at O'Connell's and write the neighborhood newspaper, the *Near North News*. The park is a place where Rush, State, and Bellevue converge.

Across the street, where the Newberry high-rise now stands was a brownstone named the Gate of Horn where folk singers like Jo Mapes, the Kingston Trio, and Bob Camp would perform. South of our apartment, on the east side of the street, was A Bit of Sweden, where they served smorgasbord. Then, down Rush Street, was The Singapore, owned by Tommy Downs, where they served the best ribs in town. Across Rush was Café Bellini, a coffeehouse, and next to it was the Carnegie Theater.

Oak Street is practically the same today as it was 40 to 50 years ago. The low rise buildings are still there, as well as some high-rises, including the one at Oak and Rush. At Michigan Avenue and Oak Street is 1000 Lake Shore Drive, a building that was considered to be the first high-rise in the area. Today, another major building, One Magnificent Mile, at Oak and Michigan, dominates the corner across the street. Walton Street, one block south, still has many buildings on the north side of the street that have been there a long time. They probably will remain intact because a lot of the building facades have been designated as landmarks, particularly on East Lake Shore Drive.

The stretch of Michigan Avenue from the Chicago River to the lakefront at Oak Street is one of the most attractive short-haul trips that one can ever take. I've walked it during the day, during the night, during different seasons; and I believe that it's there for people to use and enjoy.

left

In 1976, ribs and exotic dancers were the main draw at the Singapore Restaurant, which stood on the east side of Rush Street between Oak Street and Bellevue Place. Burlesque bars were vying with the established comedy clubs for a share of the convention and tourism business (Sigmund J. Osty photo, courtesy of the Chicago History Museum, ICHi-52283).

right

Looking east along the north side of Oak Street in 1970, the contrast between the old graystone edifices and the modern residential towers along Lake Shore Drive is abrupt (Sigmund J. Osty photo, courtesy of the Chicago History Museum, ICHi-52294).

bottom

The south side of Oak Street in 1957, with the Drake Hotel and Palmolive Building prominent in the background. The Ranch Restaurant was located in Holabird & Roche's Palmer Shops Building, completed in 1922. Today, One Magnificent Mile stands on this site (photographer unknown, courtesy of the Chicago History Museum, ICHi-52293).

above left

The most prominent landmark on Oak Street was the Esquire Theatre. Completed in 1938, it was one of the rare new buildings constructed during the Depression era. Hailed for its streamlined Moderne design, the theatre shut down in 2006 to be replaced by retail stores. This exterior photo was taken in 2008. One of the most memorable events here was the opening of *Star Wars* in 1977; the ticket line extended beyond Rush Street (Eric Bronsky photo).

above right

The sleek, uncluttered lobby as it appeared in 1938 (Hedrich-Blessing photo, courtesy of the Chicago History Museum, HB-04606-A).

right

The theatre as originally configured had more than 1,400 seats, but in 1989 it was split up into six smaller theatres (Hedrich-Blessing photo, courtesy of the Chicago History Museum, HB-04606-G).

The one-block stretch of Walton Street between Michigan Avenue and Rush Street was another center of activity. In this 1962 photo, Don the Beachcomber and The Embers stood on the south side, across the street from the Playboy Club (F.S. Daughwalter photo, courtesy of the Chicago History Museum, ICHi-52261).

Shecky Greene

When I grew up, I always thought of our downtown as beautiful because it had Grant Park, The Art Institute, and all of the city's other attractions. I actually got my big break in show business when I appeared on Rush Street. Located just a few blocks west of Michigan Avenue, it was an exciting street and included places like Mister Kelly's and the Club Alabam. The greatest thing about the Club Alabam was their sign with the dancing girl in lights kicking her leg high into the air. Of course, I believe that the Club Alabam finally went out of business because the girl couldn't get her leg up. As a matter of fact, a lot of girls couldn't get their legs up around that section of Rush Street at that time.

Happy Medium was in business at the time, just off Rush Street, and after Oscar and George Marienthal opened that place they brought in "Broadway-type" acts. The wonderful thing about it was that Anne Meara and Jerry Stiller were doing an act, although I wouldn't classify it as a comedy routine. One day I suggested to them, "Why don't you two do an act like Nichols and May?" And they started doing that, and their careers took off. I feel a little pride in that, as well as the fact that I was responsible for introducing Luciano Pavarotti on television; also the current governor of California, Arnold Schwarzenegger. So, all those people had success and I'm sitting here doing nothing.

Yet, back in the '50s and '60s, I performed at Mister Kelly's many, many times. On one occasion, Barbra Streisand was my opening act, and another time it was Helen Reddy. Mort Sahl was at Mister Kelly's a short time after me, but, as I recall, the first place he performed in Chicago was at the Black Orchid. He wasn't doing well, and Mort came to me and said, "Shecky could I borrow your tape recorder?" And, using the tape recorder that I got from Betty Hutton, Mort began to tape all of his shows to help him strengthen his act. The owners of the club wanted to fire Mort, but I went to see Al Greenfield, who owned the Black Orchid (and who was one of my best friends), and Benny Dunn, Al's right-hand man. I begged them to keep Mort on because I argued that the college kids would come to see him. Eventually they did, and he was a big success. As a matter of fact, I did such a good job of promoting Mort that my shows were empty. Shelley Berman was also performing around that same time, and he was working all over Rush Street.

Mister Kelly's was located where Gibsons restaurant is today, while around the corner on Oak Street was the beautiful Esquire Theater. The Gate of Horn was located on State Street, just to the west of Mister Kelly's. As I remember it, Rush Street had some magnificent restaurants where I may have gotten drunk occasionally, including the world famous Singapore.

Now that I am older, I can tell you that the famous Chez Paree nightclub was a real piece of garbage to work at, even though it was considered to be one of the top clubs in the country. I can say the same thing about the renowned Copacabana in New York. But, as young performers, we were frightened of those places because we were all getting our start and it was the height of one's career to work in those clubs. My first job at the Chez Paree was with Ann Sothern, but I really didn't belong there because I had no act, and it was clear that Ann didn't appreciate me. I remember that the Chez Paree brought in the big stars of the day, and it was the atypical nightclub, just like the Copacabana.

As I became more popular, I began performing at the major nightclubs across the country and it became a measure of my popularity. Then, finally, Las Vegas opened and if you performed there it meant that you were beginning to make it. It is not that way anymore because today, these kids come out of comedy clubs, do seven minutes on a television show, and they immediately become stars. I guess that's the way it should be; I don't believe that the new performers should have to go through that same tortuous route of nightclubs I was forced to endure. And besides, the average person today can no longer afford the cost of going to nightclubs.

Club Alabam was located in a onetime mansion at 747 N. Rush Street. This photo was taken in 1966 (Sigmund J. Osty photo, courtesy of the Chicago History Museum, ICHi-51452).

The Happy Medium stood at the northeast corner of Rush and Delaware Streets. Directly across the street was the Hotel Maryland (Sigmund J. Osty photo, courtesy of the Chicago History Museum, ICHi-52285).

The careers of some of the nation's most popular comedians and musicians were launched at Mister Kelly's. The Smothers Brothers and Carol Sloane were featured on the marquee when this 1963 photo was taken. The block-square building was rebuilt in the late 1960s following a disastrous fire that also gutted the Carnegie Theatre and Café Bellini. Today, the immensely popular Gibsons Bar & Steakhouse occupies the site of Mister Kelly's (Sigmund J. Osty photo, courtesy of the Chicago History Museum, ICHi-23675).

The Chez Paree was not within the Rush Street nightclub district, as it stood on the southwest corner of Fairbanks Court and Ontario Street. Nevertheless, Rush Street's biggest names also headlined this legendary club, which presided from 1932 until 1960. In 2008, the West Egg Café and Timothy O'Toole's occupied this building (Hedrich-Blessing photo, courtesy of the Chicago History Museum, HB-08380).

top

Rush and Oak Streets were for many years the site of the annual Gold
Coast Art Fair. A newspaper vendor watches the action in this August
9, 1959 view looking southeast at the Rush-Oak intersection (Marty
Schmidt photo, courtesy of the Chicago History Museum, ICHi-52306).

bottom

The same intersection, nearly forty years later, sports a new
low-rise corner building with Michigan Avenue's skyscrapers in the
background. The Gold Coast Art Fair now thrives along LaSalle Street
in the burgeoning River North neighborhood. (Eric Bronsky photo).

Phil Stefani

My childhood home was on the corner of Grand and Orleans. Right next door was Gene & Georgetti, a landmark Chicago institution since 1941. Growing up in this neighborhood, our backyard was the downtown area. I remember the State Street of old where Fritzel's and other well known places were. Sometimes we would walk to the soda fountain at the old Walgreens at State and Randolph. Later on I commuted to St. Patrick High School at Belmont and Austin. Yes, I was stuck there during the great snowstorm of '67; it took me some $9\frac{1}{2}$ hours to get home. I studied engineering at the University of Illinois in Chicago but then switched to the travel business.

We operated a travel agency at Harlem and Higgins from 1973 until 2002; I loved to travel and would go to Italy five times a year.

Having a passion for food and an uncle who was in the restaurant business, I thought this would be a good fit for me. In 1980, I bought a building at Fullerton and Southport that had a small restaurant, so I told my uncle Lino, let's give it a try. So Lino and I opened our first restaurant—Stefani's—in what was a new and coming neighborhood at the time. From there, we opened Lino's in an old warehouse building at 222 W. Ontario. And we continued to expand, opening Tuscany restaurants at several locations.

When I was a kid, I used to take the Grand Avenue bus to the end of the line and go fishing at Navy Pier. That's a nostalgic connection for me because we now have several operations at Navy Pier. In addition to our restaurant Riva, we cater private events in the Crystal Garden, the Grand Ballroom, and other venues.

I watched Rush Street change with the times. Once it was known as THE place, THE entertainment district, with all of its restaurants, clubs, and bars. But there was a period of time when places like Mister Kelly's were closing. And then, all of a sudden, a revitalization began. We opened Tavern on Rush in 1998. Other places—Gibsons, Bistrot Zinc, Carmine's and Morton's—also really helped to reenergize the whole area.

The old Riccardo's restaurant originally opened at the corner of Rush and Hubbard in 1936 and was in business until 1990 or so. A Greek family reopened it in '95, but it closed in '98. Having a lot of history, this place became of interest to us—as you know, great writers like Mike Royko and Studs Terkel frequented this location—

so in 2000, we took it over and opened Phil Stefani's 437 Rush. The old building needed a lot of work, and to conform to code, it had to be completely redone. The only thing we saved from Riccardo's was the original bar, which we restored to the way it originally looked.

And, you know, the media still frequents this location! We get a lot of people from the *Tribune* and some from the *Sun-Times*. Rick Kogan is here on a daily basis. And now I see the area around us evolving with new high-rises. The *Sun-Times* building has been replaced by Trump International Hotel & Tower, but the *Tribune* is still across the street.

I've been in the restaurant business for 28 years. It's ironic that I would come back to the neighborhood where I was born to open a restaurant. In the '50s, this was just an area of manufacturing, seamstresses, and a lot of shops, but today, the whole area has been revitalized and reenergized. Right here on Grand Avenue, hotel expansions are underway. Further west by the bridge, some sites still have low-level buildings that could end up being demolished and replaced with high-rises.

Years ago there was an exodus of people leaving the inner city to move further out, so who would ever think that the area stretching from The Magnificent Mile to McCormick Place at 22nd Street would come back? One residential high-rise after another is going up, but the mayor also wants greenery and landscaping, so there are also parks. And now they're building the Chicago Spire, which is supposed to be some 150 stories high; there's just no end to it.

Chicago is unlike many cities across the country that have died; I think the mayor has really put together a very strong city with a strong infrastructure.

O'Connell's Sandwich Shop, at the northeast corner of Rush Street and Bellevue Place, was a popular Chicago chain with several eateries around downtown (Howard B. Anderson photo, courtesy of the Chicago History Museum, ICHi-52282).

Tavern on Rush has occupied the site of the old O'Connell's since 1998 (Eric Bronsky photo).

Rush Street south of Ohio was, in 1946, a gritty secondary street overshadowed by the skyscrapers along North Michigan Avenue. Two legendary Chicago restaurants, Corona Café and Riccardo's, were then the hot spots along this otherwise unremarkable stretch (Betty Henderson photo, courtesy of the Chicago History Museum, ICHi-52262).

A colorful slice of Chicago history lives on at Phil Stefani's 437 Rush, a trendy Italian restaurant whose bar, the original from the former Riccardo's restaurant, continues to draw some of the city's most celebrated journalists (Eric Bronsky photo).

Tom Dreesen

I remember going to Michigan Avenue when I just was a little boy growing up in Harvey and shining shoes with my brother at all the local taverns. I came from a very poor family, and we had to bring money home to help feed my brothers and sisters. My mother would take a nickel from our meager earnings and put it in a little cracked cup she had in the cupboard. When she had saved enough money, she gave us some cash so that we could get on the Illinois Central Railroad and enjoy the short ride from Harvey to downtown Chicago.

My brother and I would get off at Randolph Street, roam around downtown, and that was my first introduction to this incredible place—Chicago. Being able to walk down Michigan Avenue and Randolph Street as a little boy was a true pleasure. We would see the Tribune Tower, and it was like a whole new world with all the crowds and the continual excitement.

My first introduction to Mister Kelly's happened when I was a little boy caddying for its owners, Oscar and George Marienthal, at the Ravisloe Country Club. They also owned the London House and the Happy Medium. When I first went into show business, I started going downtown a lot. In those days, Mister Kelly's was the place where all the big comedians and singers from all around the world whom you might see on the Ed Sullivan Show would perform; it was the ultimate place for those who wanted a career in show business. I also remember the Happy Medium and Punchinellos that were both on Rush Street. All the theater and show business people would eat at Punchinellos.

My career began to be shaped in the late '60s and early '70s, and I can recall all the hustle and bustle of being a new comedian and where the show business people met to have conversations. If you were lucky enough, you might be able to begin your path to stardom on Rush Street.

As a comedian, I wanted to watch other comedians perform. So, sometimes I would try to sneak into the back of Mister Kelly's and watch whoever was on stage. One time I snuck in as Mort Sahl finished his show and went to his dressing room. I decided to take the chance and try to make contact with him. I had only been in show business for about four months at the time, but I knocked on his door. He answered it alone, and I said to him, "I'm Tom Dreesen, and I am a new comedian and I just saw your show and I wondered if I could talk to you." He said, "Yeah, come on in." He was really nice to me and gave me some advice about writing jokes and preparing a stand-up routine. I remember leaving Mister Kelly's that night thinking that if I ever made it in show business and if ever a young comedian came up to me, I would also treat him with respect because Sahl had made me feel like his peer.

The excitement of Mister Kelly's in those days was that Oscar and George Marienthal had this system where they would go around the country looking for young, budding stars. A couple of those relative unknowns included Bette Midler and Barbra Streisand, who was then making no more than $250 a week at some club in New York. The Marienthals would say to such a person, "We want you to come to Chicago, and we will triple what you are making here for one week. And, the next time you come to our club, we'll double that. So, if you're making $250 a week at some club in New York, we'll give you $750 to come to Chicago. And, the next time you come back, we'll give you $1,500." Well, everybody jumped at their offer. The Marienthals knew that if they did that with someone like Bette Midler, she would work the first time, and, within a year, she would become a big star. And they had a return clause in the contract that she had to come back for $1,500. They were very smart about their business approach, but Barbra Streisand was the only one who bought out her contract for $15,000 instead of coming back. But she did perform there the first time.

The only other thing I would mention about Rush Street was Faces, another place where all the "players" of Chicago went to be seen. To tell you the truth, I couldn't afford to go in there, but once in awhile I would sneak in the back and look around. When Sinatra came to town, he would go there. Jimmy Rittenberg, one of the owners of Faces who has become a really good friend of mine, is a real Chicago guy. All those people on that strip are "Chicago guys," and Chicago guys are different from New York guys and LA guys— they are friendly, energetic entrepreneurs.

Rush Street was exciting because there was always action on that street. However, for several years when Harold Washington and Jane Byrne were mayors, Rush Street had deteriorated to the point where the street was populated with hookers, pimps, and homeless, which ruined the street for a while. But when Richie Daley became

mayor, the street came back. Look at it now because it is once again a popular, if different kind of street.

When I first went to Rush Street, it was flourishing and thriving with so much energy. You never knew who you were going to see on that street, and Mister Kelly's marquee was bold with the names of who was appearing there. If you were lucky, you might catch a glimpse of the performers coming in and out. And we got reviews in all four of the newspapers in those days.

Whenever there was a rave review, Mister Kelly's would enlarge it and put it in front of the club. So, if somebody was a big hit, it was right there for every passerby to see.

Between Rush Street and Michigan Avenue in those days was the Playboy Club on Walton. My comedy partner, Tim Reid, and I were lucky enough to perform at that famous club. In those days, the Bunnies were like young movie starlets who would come down to Rush Street after their jobs and drop in at the popular places. So, those good looking young girls could be seen all up and down Rush Street, along with the good looking young guys who were "players" driving their fancy cars, and also the "wise guys" who drove up and down the street. It was just an era of excitement. For a new kid from Harvey, that was my early introduction to show business. It was a wonderful introduction to Rush Street, and to what I considered to be the big time.

Another Rush Street comedy club, the Living Room, stood at the southeast corner of Rush and Chestnut Streets. Comedian Alan King was also a Rush Street favorite (photographer unknown, courtesy of the Chicago History Museum, ICHi-13029).

The Pit, Jim Saine's and the Tradewinds restaurants, photographed in 1951, stood together on the east side of Rush Street between Delaware Place and Chestnut Street (Roxine photo, courtesy of the Chicago History Museum, ICHi-52303).

River North and North Bridge

River North's evolution into a vibrant and thriving adjunct to The Magnificent Mile and Streeterville has been ongoing for three decades. Previously, apart from a few landmarks including Merchandise Mart and Marina City, there was little else to distinguish this long neglected neighborhood from the industrial and warehouse districts located directly across the Chicago River North Branch. But astute developers and investors saw an opportunity in this area's attractive real estate prices and easy accessibility along existing transportation corridors. The burgeoning success of North Michigan Avenue further enhanced the appeal of this area.

The opening of the East Bank Club in 1980 transformed a nondescript stretch along the riverfront into a popular destination virtually overnight. Its success helped launch the rehabilitation of nearby loft buildings into condominiums, art galleries, and interior design studios. Cafés and bars ranging from elegant to funky moved in and renovated storefronts along formerly seedy stretches of State, Clark, and Wells Streets. But it was the new tourist-oriented restaurants and nightclubs, many situated along the Ohio-Ontario corridor, which became the primary focal point of the new neighborhood.

The original boundaries of River North were considered to be LaSalle Street, Chicago Avenue, and the Chicago River, but the new neighborhood has expanded east to Rush Street/ Streeterville and as far north as Division Street.

North Bridge is not a neighborhood in the traditional sense. Literally the area just north of Michigan Avenue Bridge, in the past it was little more than the unadorned if not gritty backside of Michigan Avenue, replete with loading docks and service entrances. The stunning redevelopment of this area received a major boost from the unique Shops at North Bridge indoor mall. Shoehorned between Michigan and Wabash Avenues, the nine square block area between Ontario Street and the Chicago River is anchored by the Trump International Hotel & Tower and the Wrigley Building at the south end; and by the retail complex at 600 N. Michigan Avenue at the north end. New residential towers, upscale hotels, and some of Chicago's finest restaurants now fill out the intermediate blocks.

top

The Kinzie Street wholesale market, convenient to the Chicago River and cold storage warehouses, was one of the most important commercial areas of the Near North Side during the late nineteenth and early twentieth centuries. This view looks west from State Street (courtesy of the Chicago Transit Authority).

bottom left

Typical of the early warehouse structures was this massive building at the northeast corner of Austin Avenue and Cass Street (now Hubbard Street and Wabash Avenue) (Eric Bronsky Collection).

bottom right

This 1915 view of Ohio Street, looking east towards State Street, shows that the neighborhood a few blocks north of the river was predominantly residential. At left is the Tree Studios Building, the residence built for artists in 1894 that launched the bohemian "Towertown" community (photographer unknown, courtesy of the Chicago History Museum, ICHi-17420).

top left

Grand Avenue at Rush Street in 1929, looking northeast on a slushy
February day. The Corona Café was by then a popular establishment.
Michigan Avenue viaduct is visible in the background (Kaufmann & Fabry
photo, courtesy of the Chicago History Museum, ICHi-39353).

bottom left

In a 1948 view of the same block, looking westerly from Michigan
Avenue, the Corona Café building has shed its cornice. Owing to the
Depression and war years, little else was changed (James D. McMahon
photo, courtesy of the Chicago History Museum, ICHi-52281).

right

Some 50 years later, construction of The Shops at North Bridge would
finally revitalize this lackluster stretch of Grand Avenue. This view,
photographed from the multilevel mall entrance built directly above
Grand, looks towards Rush Street (Eric Bronsky photo).

"A section of the Near North Side was known as a "sin" area. There was gambling on Rush Street in the '60s, along with a couple of all-night bars; and along Clark Street, from Division Street all the way down to the Traffic Court, were strip joints and houses of prostitution. Where Maggiano's is located today used to be the St. Regis Hotel, and as you walked by you could hear the "melody" of creaking beds. We brought that type of business to an end in the early to mid-1970s. At the insistence of Mayor Richard J. Daley, the Chicago Liquor Commissioner and I closed down all those strip joints."
Burton Natarus

A seedy stretch of North Clark Street, looking south from Chicago Avenue, was extant in 1976 (Art Peterson photo, Peterson-Krambles Archive).

The nearly completed John Hancock Building dates this photo to the late 1960s. The old loft buildings that would eventually breathe new life into the River North neighborhood are visible beyond Marina City and the *Sun-Times/Daily News* Building (courtesy of the Chicago Transit Authority).

Grant DePorter

I was born in Seattle, and since my father worked for the Hyatt Hotels Corporation, we moved around a lot when I was young. In fact, between 1969 and 1979 we moved from Albany to Chicago to San Francisco and back to Chicago. I vividly remember our first drive from O'Hare into the city upon our return to Chicago in 1979 when my father pointed out the garbage, lack of trees, and graffiti along the Kennedy Expressway.

My sister and I became less and less excited about being back, but my father assured me by saying, "Grant, I am going to transform everything, plant trees along the expressway, and get rid of all the graffiti." He understood the importance of the first impression and knew that beautifying the routes from O'Hare and Midway into the city would have a significant impact on tourism.

My father kept his promise, and in 1986, he founded Chicago Gateway Green—a nonprofit organization dedicated to the beautification and greening of Chicago. Gateway Green really took off once Richard M. Daley became mayor in 1989, and he has remained a strong believer in the importance of "greening" and beautification. The mayor clearly and enthusiastically supported the mission and goals of Gateway Green, and when my father passed away in 1996, Mayor Daley named the entry into Chicago at Ohio, Orleans, and Ontario, the Donald J. DePorter Gateway, in honor of his dedication to greening Chicago. I also chaired Chicago Gateway Green for five years.

After living and working at the Hyatt Regency Chicago throughout high school, I decided to pursue a career in the restaurant industry. I attended the School of Hotel Administration at Cornell University, received an MBA at Duke University, and, after graduating from business

school, began working for the management group that operated Harry Caray's Restaurant along with other restaurants. Three years later, in 1990, the management group broke up and I took Harry Caray's independent. The Harry Caray's Restaurant Group now operates seven restaurants—Harry Caray's Italian Steakhouse in Chicago, Rosemont, and Lombard, Harry Caray's Seventh Inning Stretch at Midway Airport, Harry Caray's Tavern Wrigleyville, Holy Mackerel!, a fresh seafood restaurant in Lombard, and Ten Pin Bowling Lounge in Marina City.

I think that my earliest memory of River North was in 1980 when I was living in the Hyatt Regency, and the East Bank Club opened up. I used to walk from the Hyatt straight past the building that now houses Harry Caray's on Kinzie Street all the way to East Bank. Because the area was primarily filled with warehouses and industrial buildings, at certain times of day I didn't feel very safe walking there. It is amazing to see how vibrant the neighborhood has become, and I credit Mayor Daley and his encouragement of development of the area for much of its transformation. River North has been a wonderful home for Harry's—we have been busy since the day we opened, have many loyal customers, and are consistently one of the highest volume independent restaurants in the country.

The incredible dining and nightlife options of River North make it a natural nighttime attraction for visitors who spend their days enjoying the Avenue. As River North continues to grow, the synergies with North Michigan Avenue continue to develop. For example, in 1996, I volunteered to hand out the Holiday Activity Guide for The Magnificent Mile Lights Festival. I was standing in front of the Wrigley Building wearing a Harry Caray's shirt. As people passed, many saw my shirt and told me that while they had heard of the restaurant they were unsure of its exact location. I directed them to go through the Wrigley Building plaza area and continue west to the restaurant. So many people came to Harry Caray's that day, we ran out of food and had to go to the grocery store to restock! It was at that point I recognized the power of The Magnificent Mile Holiday Lights Festival, and in the late 1990s, as an active member of the Greater North Michigan Avenue Association, I became chairman of that event. These days, so many people come downtown for the event that you can't get a hotel room in the area and the restaurants are all full.

The River North area is experiencing so much expansion that construction cranes are visible from every direction of Harry's. While the areas near North Michigan Avenue have either reached or are close to reaching the point of maturity, River North still offers opportunity for major new developments including the nearly completed Trump International Hotel &Tower. The area is home to entertainment venues such as the House of Blues and Ten Pin Bowling Lounge, a wide variety of restaurants including Harry Caray's Italian Steakhouse, Smith & Wollensky, Bin 36, Ruth's Chris, and Morton's, as well as a variety of upscale hotels such as the Sax Hotel, the Westin, and the Amalfi.

When I think back to my days walking (or running) through the area to get to the East Bank Club, I have to believe that East Bank had a lot to do with the transformation of River North because it was such a prominent anchor for the area. In the future, I expect that the there will be a significant increase in the number of residential buildings in River North. However, our long-term goal is to have a good balance between residential and commercial. The area needs a combination of corporate lunchtime business, hotels, and residences to support the area's thriving night time business.

top
A vintage "red rocket" streetcar chartered by railfans on
December 18, 1955 swings around the corner at Dearborn and
Kinzie Streets, past the old Central Cold Storage warehouse.
The ornate building in the background, which would hardly elicit a
raised eyebrow back then, was destined to become one of River
North's most celebrated restaurants (William C. Janssen photo,
Peterson-Krambles Archive).

bottom
A contemporary view of the slogan-adorned Harry Caray's Restaurant
in its glory (Eric Bronsky photo).

Working an enthusiastic bar crowd at his namesake restaurant, legendary Chicago Cubs sportscaster Harry Caray serenades his ardent fans (courtesy of Grant DePorter).

Postscripts

"As a kid growing up on the city's Far North Side, my family didn't go to North Michigan Avenue for shopping or entertainment. Between Randolph and the river, it was really just a series of older office buildings along with some industrial sites off of the avenue." *Gordon Segal*

"If you had to present only one picture of Chicago that would attract tourists to come and visit our city, it would surely be a photo of North Michigan Avenue—a photo of the beautiful tulips in the median, The Magnificent Mile Lights Festival, or the range of architecturally significant buildings along the avenue." *Grant DePorter*

"North Michigan Avenue is special, and it is at the same time both elegant and popular. People are comfortable being here because it is such a people place, and they do not view the density of the area as a detractor. When planned correctly, the urban experience is enhanced." *Ralph Weber*

"Chicago's demographics are changing. At one time, Michigan Avenue had only the highest end stores, but now there seems to be a lot of variety. To have a flagship store on Michigan Avenue means something. It's still a very special place, and I think the diversity is what makes it one of the greatest avenues of the world." *Rick Roman*

"Fashionable shopping streets in other cities established long before Michigan Avenue are a clue to the future of our avenue. If our domestic and international economy remains competitive, this area should continue to evolve upward as a place where people want to live, work, eat, shop, play, and be seen. It is truly a mixed-use place, which, as time goes by, should have even better and more interesting things to offer." *James Klutznick*

"There is a great sense of community developing all around the downtown area from the Near South Side and Near West Side to the sections around Michigan Avenue and the Gold Coast. The vitality that has come to the area is just incredible." *Gordon Segal*

"Our goal is to improve this area and recognize what a great opportunity we have been given to transform a former industrial area into a residential and mixed-use neighborhood. If we don't take advantage of this opportunity, then shame on us. Now is the magical time to really do something here." *Gail Spreen*

right
A dramatic view of several of Chicago's most enduring architectural icons surrounding the Chicago River and East Wacker Drive, forming a grand entrance to The Magnificent Mile (photo by Lawrence Okrent).

Median planters and replicas of the old boulevard-style street lights enhance the appearance of the three-block stretch of North Michigan Avenue between Wacker Drive and Randolph Street. Owing to the close proximity of Millennium Park and several other cultural attractions, revitalization will inevitably occur along this stretch (Eric Bronsky photo).

A contemporary view looking north from inside the southwest tower of Michigan Avenue Bridge. The tower now houses the McCormick Tribune Bridgehouse & Chicago River Museum. One of The Magnificent Mile's newest and most unique attractions, it is open to the public from May through October (Eric Bronsky photo).

above left

The 900 N. Michigan Avenue building features an upscale indoor mall anchored by Bloomingdale's as well as the Four Seasons Hotel and condominiums. Hancock Center Plaza is in the foreground (Eric Bronsky photo).

above right

Mixed-use buildings like 900 N. Michigan Avenue (bottom-left), Hancock Center, Water Tower Place, and Olympia Centre (far right) have come to dominate a stretch of North Michigan Avenue, but maintaining a sense of openness is now a paramount focus. Note that there are no high-rise structures in the blocks between the Pumping Station and Lake Michigan. Olive Park is visible at the top of the photo (photo by Lawrence Okrent).

bottom right

Inviting pedestrian plazas, such as the two-level Pioneer Plaza adjacent to the Chicago River and the Equitable Building, help to relieve the density and monotony of closely-spaced high-rise structures (Eric Bronsky photo).

Hancock Center Plaza is just as inviting during the
holiday season as it is in warmer weather (Eric Bronsky photo).

top left

The Greater North Michigan Avenue District has also evolved into one of Chicago's foremost culinary destinations, whose restaurants serve up a wide range of cuisines in every price range. The Grand Lux Café offers upscale dining and décor with a great view from the second floor of 600 N. Michigan Avenue.

top right

The venerable Pizzeria Uno, which took over a former residence at the corner of Ohio Street and Wabash Avenue in 1943, is among the area's oldest establishments.

above

Rosebud on Rush, at the southwest corner of Rush and Superior Streets, serves Italian favorites and boisterous conviviality in a former mansion (Eric Bronsky photos).

right

A bit of Chicago legend is preserved at the original Billy Goat Tavern, tucked away on Hubbard Street at the lower level of Michigan Avenue (Eric Bronsky photos).

top left, top right, above left

The "greening" of The Magnificent Mile has resulted in a park-like setting which some believe surpasses the beauty of landscaped avenues in many other cities. Especially during the warmer season, pedestrians are less aware of being surrounded by massive buildings (Eric Bronsky photos).

above

Strolling down today's North Michigan Avenue can be a fanciful experience! The appearance and quality of retail stores along the avenue surpass other commercial streets, in part because the types of stores and the design of their facades must be consistent with local standards (Eric Bronsky photo).

Visitors to Chicago choose from a wide range of hotel accommodations like the large, luxurious, and well-located Park Hyatt or intimate but also deluxe boutique hotels such as the Whitehall, located on Delaware Avenue just off of Michigan Avenue (Eric Bronsky photos).

above left
Streeterville's skyscraper architecture as art (Eric Bronsky photo).

above right
This 2006 aerial view looking northwest spotlights the rapidly developing River East residential community within the Streeterville neighborhood. In 2008, construction began on the new Chicago Spire immediately west of Lake Shore Drive between the Chicago River and the Ogden Slip. A portion of Navy Pier is visible at the bottom right (photo by Lawrence Okrent).

bottom right
Curious pedestrians puzzle over the sight of a real New Orleans streetcar parked on Illinois Street in front of the Hotel Inter-Continental. The restored antique trolley car, visiting Chicago for just one day during 2007 to promote tourism in hurricane-torn New Orleans, portends the hope that someday a form of surface rail transit will once again provide an alternate mode of transportation within Chicago's central area (Eric Bronsky photo).

top left
The landmark Tree Studios, built on State Street between Ohio and Ontario Streets in 1894 as the center of a budding artists' colony, appeared neglected in this 1976 photo (Art Peterson photo, Peterson-Krambles Archive).

top right
The Ohio/Ontario corridor through River North is characterized by popular tourist-oriented theme restaurants such as the two-story Rock 'n' Roll McDonald's and Rainforest Café (Eric Bronsky photo).

above
The building, now part of the River North neighborhood, was magnificently restored before 2008 (Eric Bronsky photo).

Many familiar landmarks are visible in this aerial view of Chicago's renowned skyline at the north gateway to The Magnificent Mile, looking south towards Oak Street Beach and East Lake Shore Drive.

North Michigan Avenue's holiday decorations have been a Chicago institution for many decades, but beginning in 1991, GNMAA expanded this tradition into The Magnificent Mile Lights Festival featuring a parade, entertainment, and other special family events to kick off the holiday season (Eric Bronsky photos).

"I have watched Michigan Avenue as it became a reflection of us as a city and as a society. It seems to continually reflect what's great about Chicago. Sitting in Water Tower Park and looking at the old pumping station, you can't help but feel that you're part of something bigger. You think about how this avenue embodies our history and the spirit and determination of every Chicagoan. This is the city that grew from the ashes; we went from being completely wiped out to becoming a vibrant, wonderful city, which I think has more to offer than any other city in the world." *Rick Roman*

Part 7
Symposium

There are many different opinions about North Michigan Avenue—how it is today, the ways it changed throughout the twentieth century into the twenty-first century, and its future as a major avenue. It is a street of great complexity, beauty, and growth, and it has adapted to the many changes that have taken place in Chicago since 1837. Ironically, North Michigan Avenue, like Chicago itself, is a combination of being world-class and still very Midwest in nature.

North Michigan Avenue, also known as The Magnificent Mile, has been favorably compared to other avenues and boulevards in America and around the world. In fact, what has become known as the Greater North Michigan Avenue District has grown to reflect the expectations, needs, and lifestyles of Chicagoans and the many visitors to the city, in terms of shopping needs as well as the desire for upscale hotels, retail establishments, entertainment venues, restaurants, and a growing number of residential buildings. As a result, The Magnificent Mile has become an avenue for the future.

North Michigan Avenue's greatest assets are not its buildings or spectacular setting as much as the dynamic individuals who steered it in the right direction and helped it to flourish. We have assembled a panel of local business professionals to discuss present-day concerns and planning for the future of the district. These authorities represent a cross-section of civic and business interests; nearly all are members of the Greater North Michigan Avenue Association. Let's open with some general comments:

Mr. Golub: First of all, there is no other neighborhood in Chicago that will ever be able to duplicate what the Michigan Avenue-Streeterville area has accomplished. Second, it has become the top shopping concentration in the city, with a wide range of high quality retailers and department stores. Third, the North Michigan Avenue District has among the highest quality residential and office buildings in Chicago. As a result, there is a wonderful mixture of retail, residential, and office, plus a majority of the city's top five-star hotels, all concentrated in one area.

Mr. Hanig: I look at everything from the point of view of a retailer, and it has been a great experience because I essentially grew up on this avenue and watched the changes happen. For the most part, these changes have been exciting and positive, but more can be done to retain the feeling that this is a real neighborhood and not just a shopping mall.

North Michigan Avenue is favorably compared to major avenues, streets, and boulevards located in other American cities as well as those in Europe and Asia. World travelers have concluded that like the Champs Elysées, Ginza, Rodeo Drive and Fifth Avenue, the avenue is a must on an "A" list of places to visit, shop, and dine. With its floral plantings, seasonal events, and overall ambience, Chicago has become "centered" around The Magnificent Mile. But, what is unique about Michigan Avenue that sets it apart from the other great avenues of the world?

Mr. Roman: I've had the opportunity to visit other great shopping avenues, and I think The Magnificent Mile has an amazing grandeur in terms of the quality of the stores and the elegance. There is also a special quality that's hard to define. My wife says it's as though Burnham knew the best parts of the best streets in the world and put them all together in one place. We've got the architecture, character, and coziness of Paris neighborhoods; the height, beauty, and stature of New York's Fifth Avenue; and the ritzy feel and exclusivity of Rodeo Drive— a wonderful compilation of all these elements with a unique Chicago style. And it feels like a neighborhood, not just some downtown shopping center—it's wonderful!

Mr. Lagrange: Although a lot of people talk about North Michigan Avenue in terms of its retail business, I think that what has also made The Magnificent Mile so special are the buildings located to the east and west of the avenue. There is an incredible combination of places, including universities, residences, hospital, four- or five-star hotels, restaurants, and retail concentrated on and off North Michigan Avenue. The avenue is like a spine with all of the side streets that feed into it.

Mr. Julmy: Part of the avenue's appeal is the use of pleasing natural aesthetics such as the tree-lined streets, as well as the flower box planters placed in the medians. While the avenue is not as wide or impressive as the Champs Elysées, it is far better for shoppers because of the relative ease with which one can walk from one side of the street to the other.

Mr. Hanig: Michigan Avenue is an outdoor, not indoor, experience. It's a real city with real cars, real cabs, and real rain and snow, not an enclosed mall that is painted to look like a city. The maintenance and appearance of the avenue is impeccable. The flowers are changed continuously in the growing season, and people love walking down the street in all seasons.

Mr. Weber: I think one of the special physical features behind the success of the avenue is the width of the avenue and its north-south alignment. The significant open space at the Chicago River near the southern end of our district is carried north from the river and enhanced by the significant width of the avenue. This alignment and width provides a welcoming stage for the avenue's majestic buildings and the show of people experiencing the avenue.

Tourism has always been a part of Chicago, but in more recent years as Loop retail establishments, entertainment venues, and restaurants began to shift to North Michigan Avenue, visitors to the city make certain that they walk up and down the avenue. In fact, they are an integral part of the overall "picture" of the street.

Ms. Agra: I've always believed that North Michigan Avenue is a destination within a destination. Certainly anyone visiting Chicago should not miss experiencing it. Experiencing the avenue doesn't have to cost anything, and you can experience the beauty of the street, the architecture, and the planters without paying an admission fee. We tell our customers to see the rocks from famous buildings all over the world that are embedded in the Tribune Tower—that's a free experience, too. If you choose to spend significant time on the avenue, your "entrance fee" to the experience may be a hotel room or parking space.

Mr. Zwecker: Pedestrian traffic is both good and bad for North Michigan Avenue. On the plus side, such an influx of people has made it an exciting venue to see and be seen. But, the negative aspect of too many pedestrians and tourists is that there can be too much congestion for people to really enjoy the avenue.

Mr. Hanig: I'm a longtime proponent of Jane Jacobs's thoughts on what makes a vital city.[1] It is the pedestrian who drives the business on Michigan Avenue. The sidewalk and the manner in which we interact with the sidewalk is a significant part of the vitality of any city, and although the street looks beautiful today, the design has not been redone in at least 50 years.

1 Jane Jacobs is the author of *The Death and Life of Great American Cities.*

Mr. Schulman: Many changes have taken place on North Michigan Avenue over the past 10 years, and I think that they have been very positive. I am convinced that there has been a good balance of retail, restaurants, hotels, and residential development on both sides of the avenue, and I believe that the residential development has really driven the overall growth of the area during the past several years.

Ms. Spreen: Our goal is to turn the main streets into gateways into Streeterville, and we have discussed putting up fabric art, new lighting, and creating an overall fun experience that will also improve safety and security. If we can make the covered streets very bright, then the neighborhood will become even more inviting to Chicagoans and visitors.

Once, North Michigan Avenue was a street only for the "carriage trade" while the rest of Chicago and the city's tourists congregated in the Loop on State Street to be near retail icons such as Marshall Field's and Carson Pirie Scott. But as those days ended and retail establishments moved to The Magnificent Mile, so did the foot trade. More recently, the trend has been away from places like Field's, I. Magnin and Lord & Taylor to national and international chains that have impacted the avenue.

Mr. Zwecker: Ironically, Michigan Avenue today has become more like what State Street was many years ago. In fact, today, Oak Street and even Walton Street have become more focused on boutique, international and high-end stores. In addition, there are now many more hotels, with a lot of them being four- and five-star in nature and reputation, such as the Four Seasons, the Peninsula, and the Ritz-Carlton.

Mr. Hanig: Over the past 30 years, we have seen most of the local retailers along Michigan Avenue replaced with national and international chain stores. I think that's a natural course in an area where rents are rising, and there is intense interest in retail because property owners want to maximize their income. In fact, over a period of time, the rents have risen out of range for individual retailers. Both positive and negative effects have come out of this trend. The positive is international recognition of Michigan Avenue as a destination for retail shopping.

Mr. Pucci: North of the river, today's stores and merchandise really reflect European and global designs. There is no sense of 'made in America,' and more balance would certainly enhance that area. It's also interesting to note that outside corporations now own nearly all of Chicago's major banks with Northern Trust being the only holdout.

Streeterville, River North, and Rush Street are important neighborhoods located to the east and west of North Michigan Avenue. They are very much part of the past and the future of the area around The Magnificent Mile. Those neighborhoods have rich traditions that include entertainment and dining venues, shopping, medical and educational campuses, and, more recently, residential construction. The residents and businesses located in each of those smaller neighborhoods are working diligently to shape the future and how they want life to be there in the next 20-30 years.

Mr. Zwecker: I think that while Chicagoans may recognize traditional names for the neighborhoods of their youth, they don't know or understand the particular histories of places like the Gold Coast or Streeterville. In fact, Streeterville is more easily recognized as the location of Northwestern University or Northwestern Memorial Hospital as well as a series of older buildings and new high rises.

My memories of Rush Street focus on what I perceived as a "naughty" place during the '60s and '70s. In fact, I remember going to some of those bars, entertaining people there, and knowing that drinks were "watered" and that prostitutes prowled the street. There was a little bit of danger to the area, as well some excitement at places like The Candy Store, Singapore, and Club Alabam. And, sadly, Mister Kelly's and Sweetwater were already closed before I was old enough to go there, although I was able to go to the Carnegie Theatre, Gate of Horn, and The Happy Medium.

As North Michigan Avenue fills up more of its available land, there has been a slow but steady movement back south of the Chicago River where the city had its first development. New developments at Lake Shore East, Millennium Park, Grant Park, The Art Institute of Chicago, the new downtown, and as far south as the Museum Campus are working with the city to plan for their future.

Mr. Pucci: Michigan Avenue is really the spine of Chicago. But south of the river, the avenue has been neglected. The three-block stretch between Wacker and Randolph Streets, especially, has no charisma and makes no statement; it's just a bunch of buildings, that's all. When Millennium Park was built, the city should have made this a port of entry by continuing the landscaping from the park to the river. But this stretch is so dark and dreary that people tend to avoid it.

True, during the Burnham era and later, some wonderful architectural masterpieces were created here. Besides the 333 N. Michigan building, there's the London Guarantee Building and the Union Carbide and Carbon Building—which today houses the Hard Rock Hotel—on the west side of the street. But after the war, the avenue north of the river began to develop and what should have remained an important corridor south of the river began to deteriorate. It could have been developed into something beautiful, but instead we got Illinois Center, which is just a bunch of box-shaped buildings. Someday, they will end up tearing down many of the older structures on these blocks and redeveloping the land because it's so valuable. Only then would Michigan Avenue south of the river have any chance of resuming its old role as the premier street in Chicago.

Mr. Carlins: I think that as North Michigan Avenue started to grow with the addition of higher end stores, it started to become the "Michigan Mile" (later "The Magnificent Mile") as stores filled in. More recently, it has probably experienced its highest reputation. Now, when stores, hotels, and businesses first come to Chicago, their first priority and mindset is to try to be located on North Michigan Avenue rather than South Michigan Avenue. The river is basically a demarcation, although it is starting to change as more development comes south and as most of them cannot get a street site. In that way, South Michigan Avenue is beginning to gain momentum, and a lot of the buildings along that part of Michigan Avenue are historic.

All portions of North and South Michigan Avenue have been forced to deal with the issues of congestion and density in terms of too many people, too much traffic, not enough parking facilities, and too much construction. Some feel that density is not a major concern, while others argue that it is the single most important issue to be faced in the near future.

Mr. Weber: This area will continue to deal with the density issue. In a way, Northwestern Memorial, with the addition of Children's Memorial Hospital, has become somewhat of a "hole in the donut" because our buildings are only about 23-24 stories high. We bring a lot of people to the area because our facilities draw an increasing number of patients and visitors, and that means more cars and traffic.

Ms. Hefner: My greatest concern about the area east of North Michigan Avenue, long-term, is the increasing amount of traffic congestion as a result of the rapid growth of residential structures, the expansion of the many hospital buildings, and new commercial construction. I am not certain that the area's infrastructure can handle all this growth. It is not as if the city is going to widen North Michigan Avenue or the side streets to accommodate the increase in traffic. But despite such concerns, these problems are not unique to Chicago since other major cities face similar challenges as their core neighborhoods continue to expand.

Ms. Spreen: In Streeterville, we are seeking to encourage people to walk and bike. Although we will always have traffic here, the city feels that since Illinois and Grand are wide thoroughfares, they will continue to be able to handle a lot of throughput. There is also the opinion that both streets are underutilized at this time. One suggestion has been to consider other ways to bring people into and out of the neighborhood.

This includes using the river more because it is our greatest untapped resource and allowing those who take the trains into the city to connect to things like the Wendella boats to get here. We also want to improve the experience of taking trolleys and walking through the neighborhood. The trolleys are fantastic, they're free, and people feel safe when they use them.

Mr. Stefani: I'm just amazed at North Michigan Avenue's growth and how well it looks. It really doesn't appear to be boxed in, overdeveloped, or overly congested as some critics say. I think the avenue moves very well compared to some other major cities. And, if you look at the cost of parking here compared to other major cities, it is still very reasonable.

Ms. Agra: I hope that I live to see the day when there is some type of ecologically friendly streetcar-type transportation to circulate people between the south end of the Cultural Mile and the north end of The Magnificent Mile.

Mr. Zwecker: I live in the Streeterville neighborhood, and that allows me to be an onsite observer as North Michigan Avenue goes through its many changes. I have mixed feelings about whether these changes are good for the city even though they are bringing traffic to the businesses that are there, and such influx is good for the restaurants, stores, and hotels. However, I do think that there are times when it becomes so congested that there is a definite problem with too much vehicular traffic, especially on the side streets.

Mr. Roman: Just as people become victims of their own success, some of the by-products of this area's popularity can make it difficult to enjoy the Avenue. The original planners and developers of North Michigan Avenue surely had no idea that it would become such a great destination. Auto traffic seems to get harder to manage every year. And, as for pedestrian traffic, there are times when it's so elbow-to-elbow tight, if you picked your feet up, the crowds could carry you!

The issue of "greening" has taken on greater importance in recent years. Two of the leaders on this topic have been Gordon Segal of Crate & Barrel and Robert Wislow of U.S. Equities, who, along with support from the city and the Greater North Michigan Avenue Association, have worked diligently to brighten the avenue and make The Magnificent Mile into a place that tourists and local citizens can enjoy from season to season.

Ms. Agra: Without a doubt, it's the greening of the street—the sidewalk and median planters—that makes North Michigan Avenue stand out from other urban shopping districts. And it's walkable, friendly, and clean. Block after block offers window shopping or hotel lobbies to rest in.

Ms. Spreen: While we don't want to copy what Gordon Segal has done on North Michigan Avenue, we are always encouraging the use of flowers, although we don't want to mandate certain planters. We are seeking to have a cohesive theme and feel throughout the neighborhood that can be sustained.

Finally, one of the biggest questions facing those who live and work in and around North Michigan Avenue as well as city leaders is: What is the future of The Magnificent Mile and its adjacent neighborhoods? There are many viewpoints, but overall, the future appears to be very positive.

Mr. Klutznick: Chicago is a great international city, but a bargain compared to New York, Tokyo, London, Paris, or Hong Kong. While Michigan Avenue's rents range up to $300-400 per square foot, other streets of the world reach up to $1,000 per square foot and beyond. The devaluation of the American dollar makes everything even more of a bargain to foreign stores and visitors, and as a result, more of them are locating and shopping in Chicago and other American cities.

Fashionable shopping streets in other cities established long before Michigan Avenue are a clue to the future of our avenue. If our domestic and international economy remains competitive, this area should continue to evolve upward as a place where people want to live, work, eat, shop, play, and be seen. It is truly a mixed-use area, which, as time goes by, should have even better and more interesting things to offer.

Mr. Golub: There are going to be more condominium and hotel developments in and around North Michigan Avenue and Streeterville as young people and empty nesters are moving downtown in greater numbers. Overall, the area is an environment of easy living.

Chicagoans care about the city's future. The key is that the city has established a close partnership between business, industry, and political leaders, which is very unique for a major metropolitan area. So, the motto is true: Chicago is the city that works.

Mr. Julmy: It is clear that the Greater North Michigan Avenue Association (GNMAA) has played a major role in the development of the avenue from the days it was established in 1912 to the late '40s when it was led by Chicago developer Arthur Rubloff, who coined the name "The Magnificent Mile." Today, GNMAA continues to preserve, promote, and enhance the neighborhood into a most unique and dynamic urban community, and make "The Magnificent Mile" one of the great avenues of the world.

PHOTO INDEX

SUBJECT INDEX